Coastal Walks

The South-west Peninsula Coast Path

1 Minehead *to* St Ives

D1783735

by Ken Ward and John H N Mason

Letts **Guides**

Charles Letts & Company Ltd.
London, Edinburgh and New York

Contents

First published 1977 by
Charles Letts and Company Limited
Diary House, Borough Road, London SE1 1DW
Cover and design: Ed Perera
Maps: Ian Ward

© Ken Ward and John H N Mason

ISBN 0 85097 258 2

Printed in Great Britain by
Letts Erskine Limited, Dalkeith

Introduction

Book 1 170 miles of Coastal Walking

The South-west Peninsula Coast Path is unique; a walk of 500 miles through some of the finest coastal scenery in Europe.

Starting unpretentiously in a passage-way off Minehead Harbour it strides across the rich cliff tops of Somerset and North Devon, scrambles over the rocky shores and beetling cliffs of Cornwall, meanders through the sailing and holiday centres of South Devon and, after crossing the airy cliffs of Hardy country, finishes among the sand hills of Studland.

It is a rich tapestry this coastline, offering to the walker a variety of terrain unsurpassed by any of the other long-distance paths. Some of it is as challenging (and exhausting) as anything to be found on the Pennine Way or on the Fells. The ascent to the bare windswept summit of the Great Hangman which looms 1000ft above the boiling seas below or the scramble to the airy top of Houns-tout cliff with its eagle eye prospect of the Dorset coast should be enough to tempt the most ardent devotee of the Fells. Again, some of it would tempt the seaside holidaymaker into exploring.

The distinct advantage that the Coastal Path has over the Northern paths is the temperate climate of the South-west, which extends the walking period to late winter and early spring —in two years of out-of-season walking we counted wet days on the fingers of one hand.

Cornwall in the early spring is a dream: lonely cliffs and empty beaches, riots of daffodil and rhododendron, and long evenings to be spent sampling the local ale and gossip.

There is much else to distract and absorb the walker on this Coast. The peoples of this distinctive part of Britain have turned their hands to many pursuits in the cause of survival. The delightful fishing harbours remain as a tribute to the hardy generations of pilchard and mackerel fishers. The gaunt empty engine houses of the tin mines which stand sentinel on the Cornish cliffs provide a melancholy reminder of the industry's meteoric rise and fall.

The naturalist has a particular treat in store. The cliffs and sands are rich in flora and wildlife that have been driven from inland pastures by intensive modern agriculture. Its role as front line defence of the island has left this coastline rich in reminders of invasions that never came, striking an incongruous note in a harmonious and tranquil scene.

Although originally mooted some twenty years ago the path remains very much in a development state. Certain sections have been impeccably waymarked and cleared, other stretches are unmarked and overgrown. In producing this series of guides we have sought to provide the prospective walker with sufficient information and guidance to enable him to find even the most neglected paths.

How to use the Book

Walking the path

In some places the path is clearly signposted and easily followed, notably in National Trust areas. In others it may be less well marked and maintained but with the guide you should always find the route. The recommended path is shown as a solid green line. Alternatives are shown as broken lines.

Italics are used in the text to denote diversions from the walk itself, for instance comments on places of interest.

The sketch maps

The sketch maps are in no way designed to supplant the excellent series of Ordnance Survey Maps (1 : 50,000) and the walker is strongly recommended to provide himself with these. Appropriate reference numbers of the OS Maps are included in the diagrams on pages 6 and 7.

Distances

On the right-hand side of the maps an indication of approximate mileage is given.

Half-day walks or treks of several days

In preparing this guide we have sought to cater for everyone with an interest in the Path. Accordingly, with the guide, it is possible for the more serious walkers to spend a week or fortnight walking continuously. Equally it is possible for those whose interest extends only to an afternoon stroll to use the guide to select an appropriate stretch. To help in this we have included on the maps the most convenient access points to the Path, usually with adjacent car parking facilities.

Bus services Many are seasonal and others irregular. Always check locally. Bus time-tables are a help. Western National, Queen Street, Exeter (0392) 74191 will tell you which you need.

Refreshments Many refreshment places are only open June–August.

Bathing Often dangerous, particularly for non-swimmers. Be guided by flags and lifeguards.

Accommodation

The accommodation shown in the guide has been selected for its position close to the Path and capacity to provide overnight bed and breakfast.

Most have become known to the authors in the two years of walking and research that have gone into producing this guide, and we offer them in good faith without accepting responsibility for them.Some are excellent, some provide a reasonable service.

We have divided the accommodation into two price categories. The higher price range is indicated by a bed with knobs on. However when making reservations always check the costs.

No addresses are given but the information should be enough for postal location. Telephone numbers are given in every case so that you can call and ask for directions. As far as possible we have tried to indicate on the maps their approximate position in relation to the path. We recommend that you decide each evening your target for the following day and then book the nearest suitable accommodation to it. If they are full, ask them to suggest an alternative; you will find them all most helpful. Always check the price; always make clear whether or not you require an evening meal; and try to give some indication of the expected time of your arrival.

Two letters after the name indicate the period that accommodation is available, eg AO = April to October, SM = September to March, ie winter only. ☐ indicates that the place is open throughout the year including the winter months. However this is subject to, as one host put it, 'our week's holiday, the annual paint and spring clean and burst pipes!'

Book 1 This book covers the sector from Minehead to St Ives. As, at the time of writing, there is no continuous path for most of the way between Saunton and Hartland Point this part of the coast is omitted. The Countryside Commission, John Dower House, Crescent Place, Cheltenham, Gloucestershire, GL50 3RA will advise you of the latest situation on this stretch. The other two books in the series cover St Ives to Plymouth and Plymouth to Poole Harbour.

Index to Sections

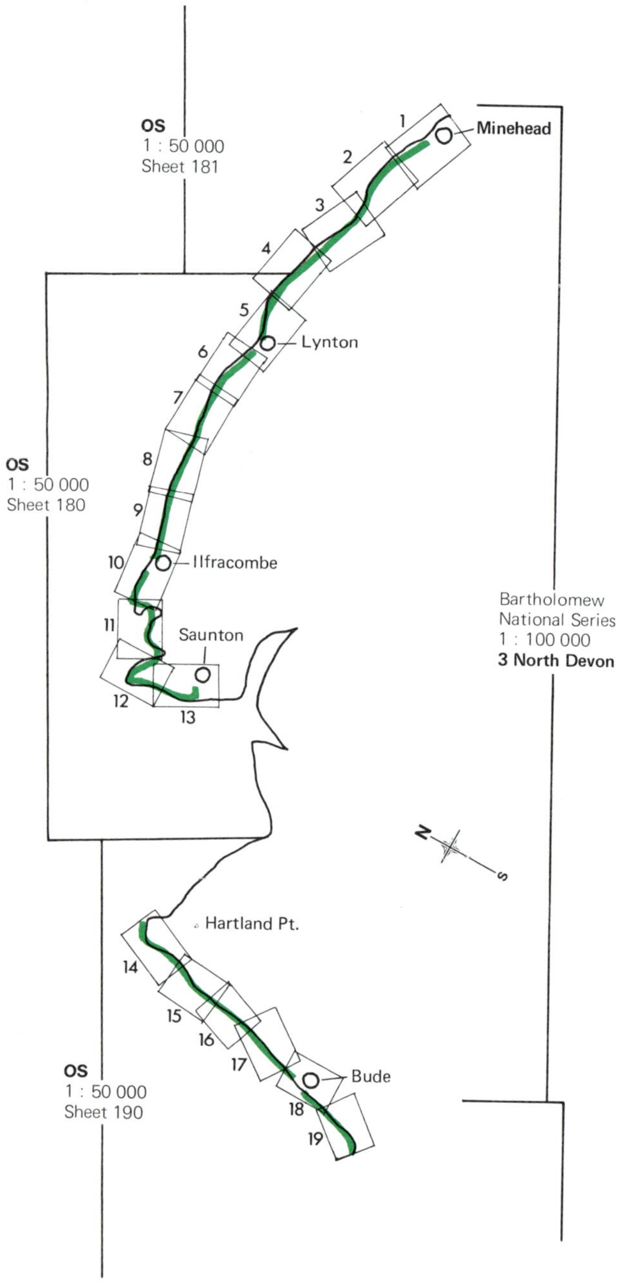

OS
1 : 50 000
Sheet 181

1
2
3
4

Minehead

5
6 — Lynton
7
8
9
10 — Ilfracombe

OS
1 : 50 000
Sheet 180

11
Saunton
12
13

Bartholomew
National Series
1 : 100 000
3 North Devon

N
S

14
Hartland Pt.
15
16
17
18
19

Bude

OS
1 : 50 000
Sheet 190

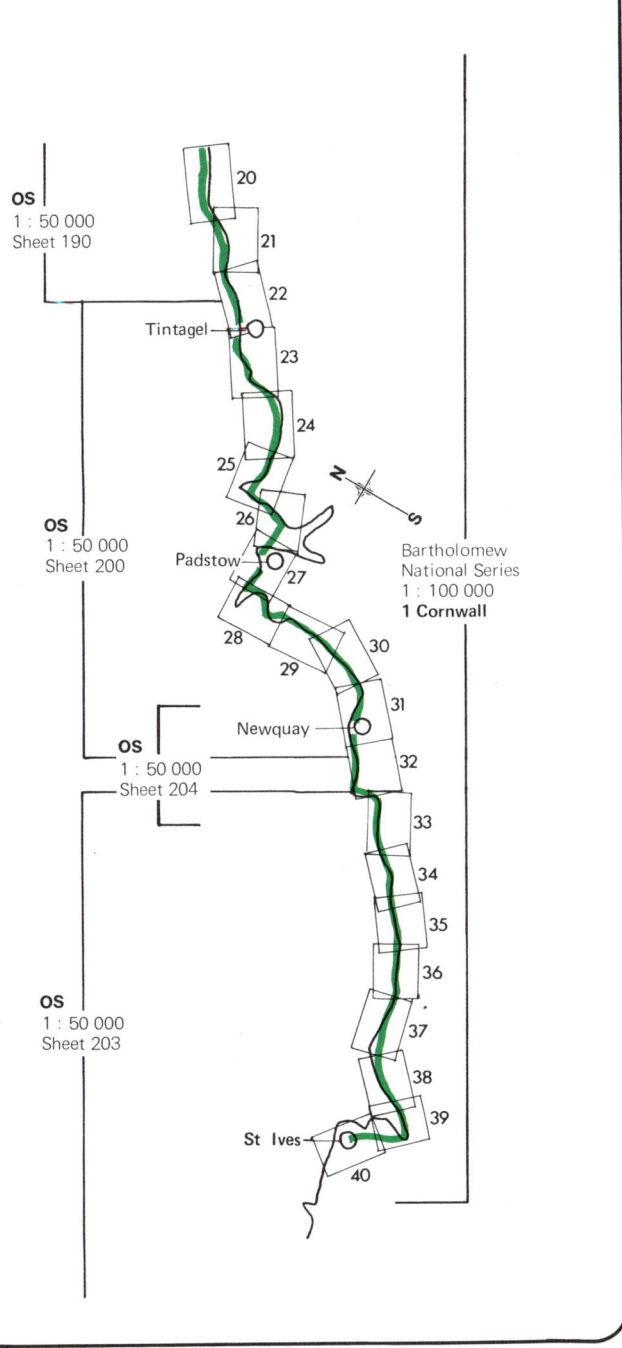

OS
1 : 50 000
Sheet 190

20
21
22

Tintagel

23

24

25

26

N

S

Padstow

27

28

29

30

OS
1 : 50 000
Sheet 200

Bartholomew
National Series
1 : 100 000
1 Cornwall

Newquay

31

32

OS
1 : 50 000
Sheet 204

33

34

35

36

OS
1 : 50 000
Sheet 203

37

38

39

St Ives

40

Tides

When walking the South-west Peninsula Coast Path a knowledge of the state of the tide on a particular day is often useful. On stretches covered by other books in this series you may have to wade an estuary and this can only be done at low tide.

The table given below will enable you, with the help of your newspaper, to determine the approximate time of high and low water. You may also be able to buy local tide tables at newsagents.

Most national daily papers give the time of high water at London Bridge (usually with the weather details). By adding to this the average time difference in hours and minutes given in the following table you can calculate the approximate time of high water at the places mentioned. For intermediate places the time will be at some time between the two places each side.

Low water is approximately 6 hours after high water.

	hrs	min
Porlock Bay	**4**	**32**
Ilfracombe	**4**	**17**
Appledore	**4**	**13**
Budehaven	**3**	**55**
Padstow	**3**	**42**
Newquay	**3**	**33**
St Ives	**3**	**32**

Tidal predictions given above are computed by the Institute of Oceanographic Sciences, copyright reserved.

Pub opening times

Pub opening times can vary from district to district and from town to town and it is impossible to give information that applies everywhere. The following should, however, serve as a general guide to places on our sector of the Coast Path.

Monday to Saturday	10.30—14.30
	17.30 –22.30*
Sundays	12.00—14.00
	19.00—22.30

*Usually open until 23.00 on Fridays and Saturdays and on other weekdays June to September.

Symbols

Access to path	Feature (see text)
Path	Parking
Alternative	Toilets
Other footpaths	Telephone
Steeply up	Shop
Steeply down	Meals
Fence	Light Refreshments
Hedge or wall	Pub
S Stream	Pub specially recommended
G Gorse	Bed and breakfast lower to medium price range
B Bracken	Bed and breakfast more expensive
Footbridge	all above
Rocks near path	
Paving stones	Open all year
'Trig' point	Camp site
NT National Trust	Overnight pitch if permission obtained
CG Coast Guard	Church with tower
Shingle or sand	Church with spire
Rocks or boulders	Ferry
Good beach	Railway Station
Swimming	Bus station
Surfing	Bus stop
Lighthouse	Birds or flowers
Incline	

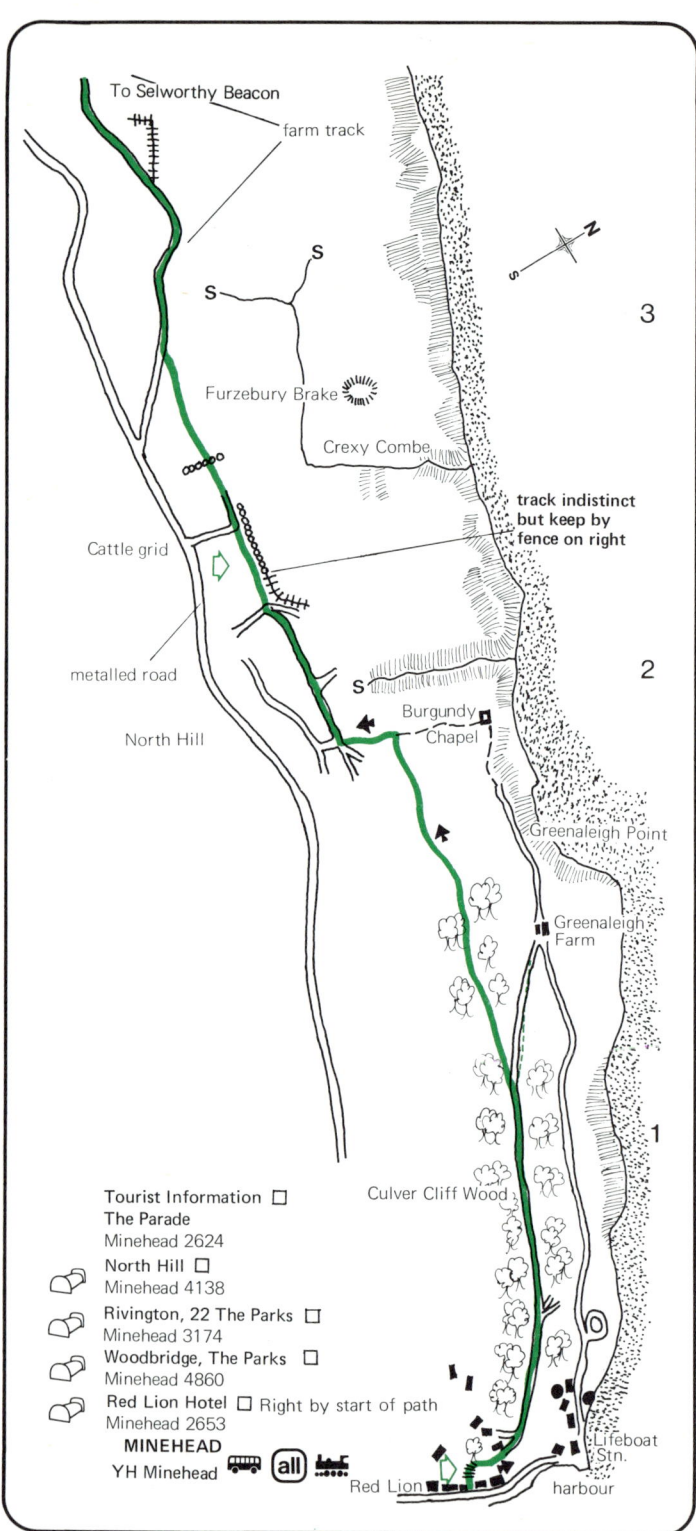

To Selworthy Beacon

farm track

S

S S

N

3

Furzebury Brake

Crexy Combe

**track indistinct
but keep by
fence on right**

Cattle grid

2

metalled road

S

North Hill

Burgundy
Chapel

Greenaleigh Point

Greenaleigh
Farm

1

Culver Cliff Wood

Tourist Information ☐
The Parade
Minehead 2624

North Hill ☐
Minehead 4138

Rivington, 22 The Parks ☐
Minehead 3174

Woodbridge, The Parks ☐
Minehead 4860

Red Lion Hotel ☐ Right by start of path
Minehead 2653

MINEHEAD

YH Minehead 🚌 (all) 🚂

Red Lion

Lifeboat
Stn.

harbour

1. Minehead-Selworthy Beacon

3½ miles 5½km

Going: after a steep climb out of Minehead itself the Path rises more gradually to a level, exposed, high moorland walk. The going is good. There are no facilities for refreshment before Porlock (6 miles) except at Selworthy or for tea at Bossington (section 2).

Minehead (pop 8250) is the chief resort of West Somerset. The name is possibly Celtic meaning 'settlement below the hill', an apt description. All facilities; sandy beach with safe bathing. Information Office: 5 The Parade. Old Minehead— by the Harbour and in Higher Town 300ft above—has great charm, with its narrow streets and lime-washed cottages. The tower of the 15th-century St Michael's church dominates the scene. Its treasures include two old brasses and a 500-year-old illuminated missal (service book) that belonged to a 15th-century vicar who became Bishop of London. Another Minehead distinction is its privately owned railway, partly steam-hauled, to Taunton.

The 500-mile South-west Peninsula Coast Path starts inconspicuously but attractively between old cottages on the Harbour (Quay St) a few yards beyond the Red Lion pub. A sign directs to North Hill and to the Coast Path which goes round the flank of the Hill.

There is a North Hill Nature Trail. Details from the Information Office in Minehead.

The Path climbs steeply zig-zagging up to Culver Cliff Wood (sessile oak, conifers, sycamores and holly). A sign shows you are entering the Exmoor National Park which extends 35 miles along the coast and 15 miles inland (information from 5, The Parade). You then come to a rhododendron area, resplendent in early summer. The Path emerges into the open above Greenaleigh Farm allowing fine views over the sea.

½ mile farther on a sign directs on the seaward side of the Path to the Burgundy Chapel. The few stones crowning a knoll that can be seen from the Path are all that remain of a chapel of unknown origin—it may have been a votive chapel put up by a pious landowner. The derivation of the name is also a mystery.

Gradually climbing higher, the Path reaches 800ft when crossing wild exposed moorland. It changes direction once or twice.

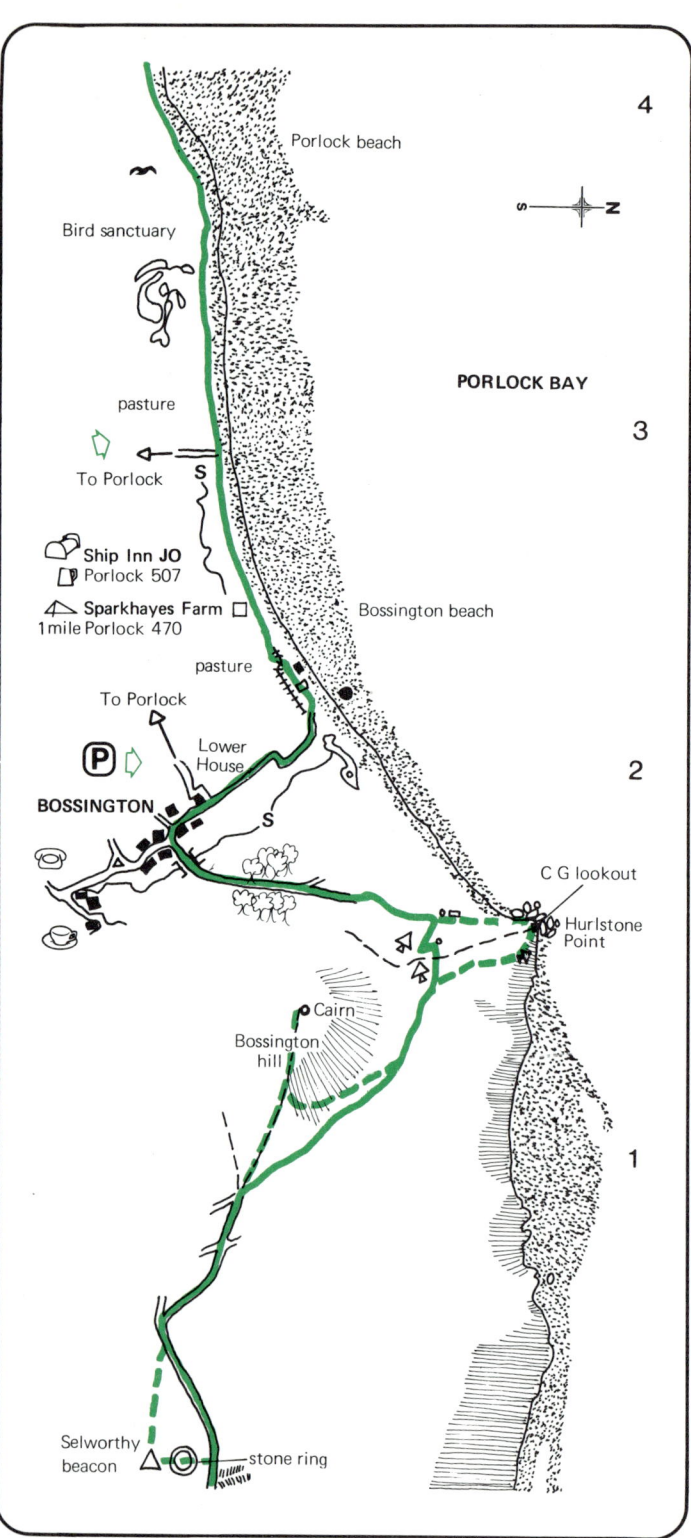

Porlock beach

Bird sanctuary

pasture

To Porlock

S

PORLOCK BAY

Ship Inn JO
Porlock 507

Sparkhayes Farm
1 mile Porlock 470

Bossington beach

pasture

To Porlock

P

Lower House

BOSSINGTON

S

C G lookout

Hurlstone Point

Cairn

Bossington hill

Selworthy beacon

stone ring

2. Selworthy Beacon-Porlock Beach

4 miles 6½km   From Minehead 7½ miles 12km

Going: a steep descent from 900ft to sea-level and then on the level by lane, country road, and beach track. After about 1 mile beyond the Burgundy Chapel you come abreast of Selworthy Beacon (1013ft).

The diversion to the summit of Selworthy Beacon on which there is a cairn and Trig Point is worthwhile for its splendid views of the coast and Exmoor. Below you, 1 mile inland to the south, is Selworthy, picture-book village owned by the National Trust.

Shortly after the signpost below Selworthy Beacon the Path begins its steep descent over the turf.

Two diversions can be made before you reach the bottom: Bossington Hill whose cairn-topped summit can be seen left of the Path; and from half-way down, along a path marked dangerous, Hurlstone Point for views of the beetling cliffs.

From the bottom of the steep slope the Path continues along a pleasant farm track which crosses a footbridge over the stream to Bossington.

Bossington is another Somerset gem, where the phone box seems the only thing less than 300 years old. A few minutes suffice to explore its one street: old cottages, Lower Lynch Farm and medieval chapel of ease. Refreshments at the Old Bake House.

The route of the Coast Path turns seaward along the narrow road from the village, past Lower House. Near the sea a sign points the way over the fields and a series of stiles, below the bank of shingle stretching 2 miles to Porlock Weir.

Just beyond Lower House a footpath takes you across fields to Porlock where you can find cafés, restaurants and pubs, old houses and cottages, and a church, much of which dates from before 1360. Its dedication, improbably, is to a St Dubricius who apparently was a 7th-century Welsh missionary monk. The effigies of a 14th-century knight in armour and a 15th-century lord of the manor are most moving. Another footpath leading off the main street just before the start of the precipitous Porlock Hill, will take you back to the coast path.

As you progress below the bank of shingle, inland of the Path is Porlock Marsh, a bird sanctuary. This is a favourite area for numerous waders on spring and autumn passage, as well as ducks in winter (see chapter on birds, p 93).

13

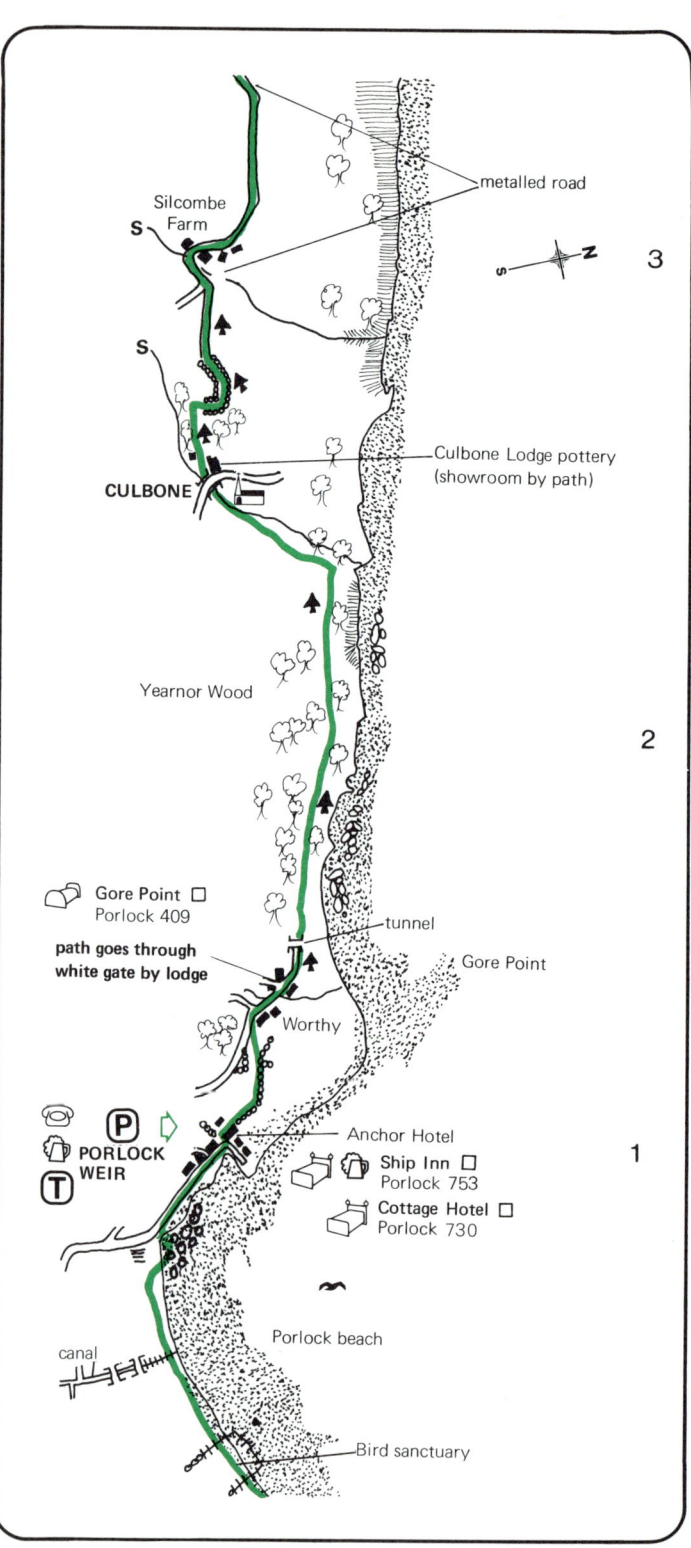

metalled road

Silcombe Farm

S

S

CULBONE

Culbone Lodge pottery (showroom by path)

Yearnor Wood

Gore Point □
Porlock 409

path goes through white gate by lodge

tunnel

Gore Point

Worthy

PORLOCK WEIR

Anchor Hotel

Ship Inn □
Porlock 753

Cottage Hotel □
Porlock 730

Porlock beach

canal

Bird sanctuary

3

2

1

3. Porlock Beach-Silcombe

3½ miles 5½km   From Minehead 11 miles 17½km
Going: varied, with stony beach, field track, woodland path and farm road. Going good, except for the short stretch of beach.

The field path behind the shingle bank of Porlock beach finishes, leaving you to walk for a short distance over the big stones of the beach itself and then for a few yards on the road to Porlock Weir, a charming hamlet.

Formerly a busy port, Porlock Weir was engaged, like Minehead, in trade with Wales across the Bristol Channel, bringing in coal and sending back pit props from the woods behind. The 'Weir' seems to be used here in its old English meaning of shelter or harbour wall. The few cottages and the 16th-century inn, The Ship, must still look as they did two or three centuries ago but the yachtsman and the holidaymaker have replaced the sailor and shipper.

The Path is signposted at the back of the Anchor Hotel (there is also a right-of-way in front of the hotel which joins the Path up some steps). You cross pleasant fields to the toll gate at Worthy, an estate of ancient foundation. Motorists can reach Lynmouth by the toll road without having to ascend steep Porlock Hill (A39). As a pedestrian you pass through the white gate without charge, the Path climbing steadily through oak woods until you suddenly come upon the Culbone church.

An amusingly written leaflet on sale inside this dimunutive church gives its history and draws attention to some unique features, one of which is its appearance in two famous Record Books: William the Conqueror's Domesday Book, and the Guinness Book of Records! It claims to be the smallest church in Britain in which services are still performed. Nearby is the Culbone Pottery and this and the church are now the only buildings left of a village which up to 100 years ago was of some importance. Charcoal burning was the main occupation carried out apparently by lepers.

A short climb after leaving the church and you come out on a wide well-surfaced farm road through pastureland, dropping down to the sea which is out of sight. You soon come to Silcombe Farm perched at the head of a deeply sided coombe.

In this type of steep open country buzzards may often be seen and you may spot one wheeling high in the air in search of prey.

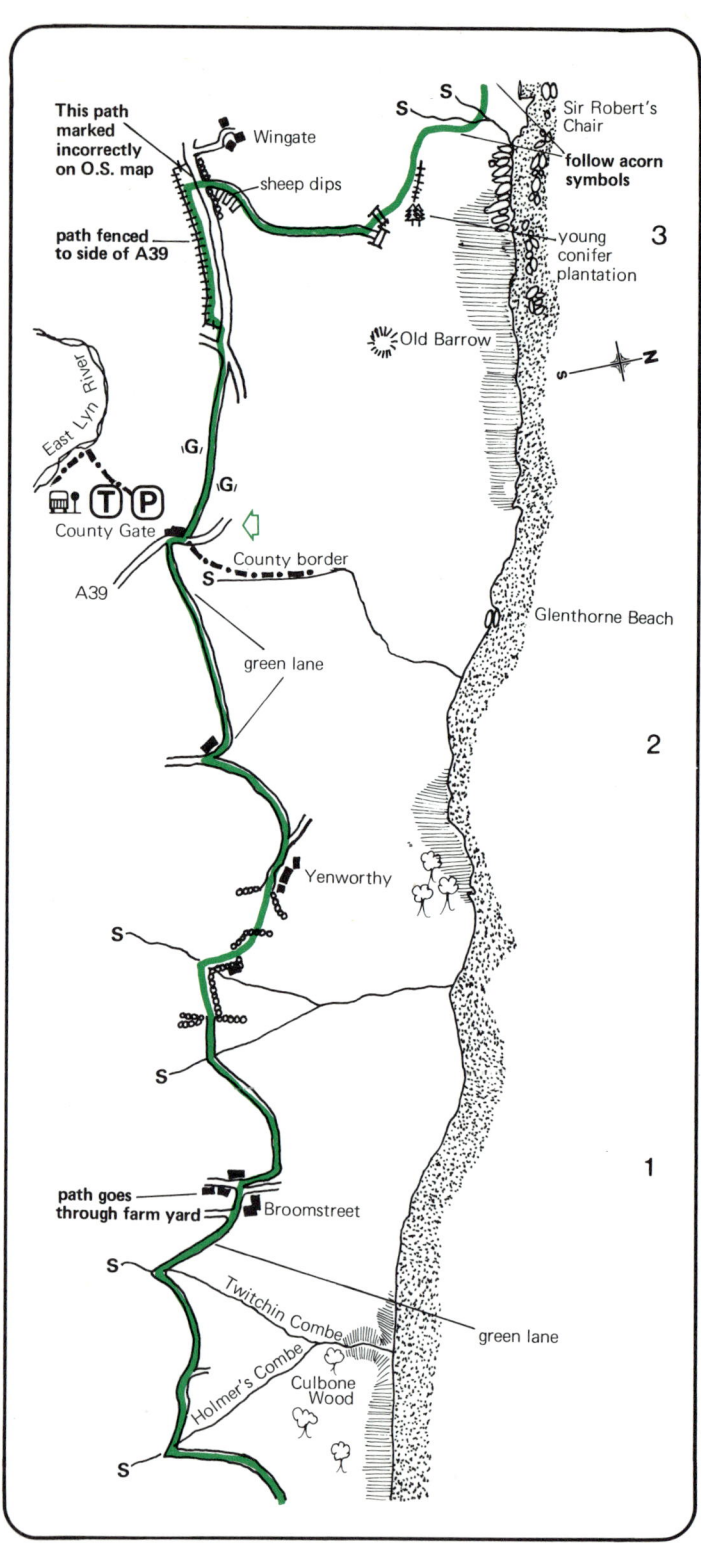

This path marked incorrectly on O.S. map

Wingate

sheep dips

path fenced to side of A39

East Lyn River

\G/

\G/

County Gate

A39

County border

green lane

Yenworthy

S

S

path goes through farm yard

Broomstreet

S

Twitchin Combe

Holmer's Combe

Culbone Wood

green lane

S

S

S

Sir Robert's Chair

follow acorn symbols

young conifer plantation

3

Old Barrow

S

Z

Glenthorne Beach

2

1

4. Silcombe-Wingate

3¾ miles 6km From Minehead 14¼ miles 23½km

Going: along a metalled farm track for most of the way and then over the Devon border to the start of some real cliff walking, by a twisting path, sometimes narrow. The going is reasonable except perhaps in wet weather when the Path can be slippery. It is well signposted.

Continuing along the metalled road that brought you past Silcombe Farm you pass through the yard of Broomstreet Farm and after about another ¾ mile come to Yenworthy Farm. *The three farms, Silcombe, Broomstreet and Yenworthy, all seem to be about 100 years old; looking after herds in the pastures of the steep combes on which they are situated must be quite a task. You are out of sight of the sea on most of this stretch but you have a chance of seeing at close quarters the farmer at work in a countryside full of charm.*

After Yenworthy Farm the road crosses Yenworthy Common and by taking the track over the common which runs to the seaward of a large house, you come out on the main road by the small cottage, County Gate, on the border between Somerset and Devon (large car park and refreshments in the summer).

There is a Nature Trail starting at County Gate and running 1000ft down to Glenthorne Beach. The length of the circular route is 3 miles; pamphlet from County Gate.

From County Gate the Path tops a slight rise by the side of the road and, dropping down, rejoins the road by a fenced track running alongside for about ½ mile; at the end of this path the continuation will be seen on the other side of the road.

The Exmoor National Park authorities have well signposted the Path from here; it runs over fields towards the sea and then turns west to cross a small stream flowing down a wooded combe.

On the hill, Old Barrow (1100ft), to the right (N) of the Path, trace has been found of a 1st-century Roman signal station. Its purpose is thought to have been to keep watch on the Welsh coast on the other side of the Bristol Channel but it was abandoned after a few years probably when the tribes in Wales had been conquered. There is a similar site at Martinhoe (section 7).

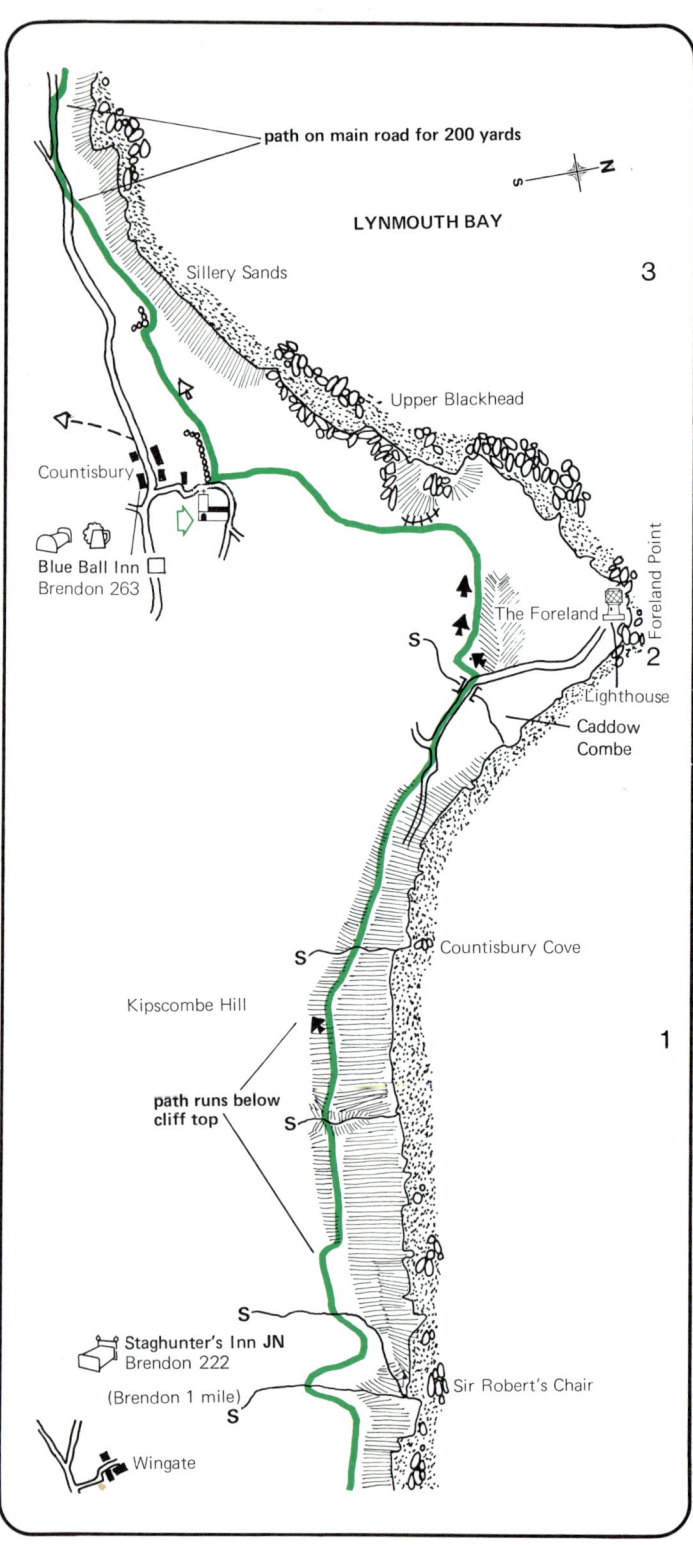

path on main road for 200 yards

LYNMOUTH BAY

3

Sillery Sands

Upper Blackhead

Countisbury

Blue Ball Inn
Brendon 263

The Foreland

Foreland Point

2

Lighthouse

Caddow
Combe

Countisbury Cove

Kipscombe Hill

path runs below
cliff top

Staghunter's Inn JN
Brendon 222

Sir Robert's Chair

(Brendon 1 mile)

Wingate

1

5. Wingate-Foreland Point-Lynmouth Bay

4¼ miles 7km   From Minehead 19 miles 30½km

Going: at first, narrow paths clinging to hillsides that drop steeply down to the sea bring you scenes as spectacular as any on the coast. The paths are quite safe for the reasonably sure-footed but care is needed in wet weather. Near Foreland Point the scenery is less dramatic but a steep climb brings you 1000ft above Lynmouth Bay with magnificent views.

The coast Path, well signposted and waymarked, is cut into the hillside sloping steeply down to the sea, and runs for about ¾ mile through woods of wind-stunted sessile oak, crossing a number of small streams.

As mentioned, this is a spectacular part of the Path—the towering cliffs, the dip of the steep slope, with the sea beneath often lashed by the strong winds—all combine to produce an unforgettable scene.

You emerge on to the narrow roadway leading through a miniature gorge, Caddow Combe, to the lighthouse on Foreland Point (open to visitors on weekday afternoons). The Path climbs out of Caddow Combe and then round Butter Hill (960ft)—you get nearly blown off your feet if there is a wind. This is National Trust land.

Eventually you come in sight of the church tower of Countisbury and the small hamlet, with its welcome pub, the Blue Ball.

Next door to the Blue Ball, stone farm buildings have been converted by the National Trust into their impressive modern Base Camp Exmoor, used by parties of young people on the Trust's working holidays— and also for adult holiday groups. The Warden will gladly show you round.

The Path runs just seaward of the church down Countisbury Hill until for the last 200 yards it has to take to the road (care needed). You can cut through a small park on the right down to Lynmouth Beach.

A fine alternative down to Lynmouth is to take the footpath off the main road just beyond the Base Camp Exmoor, signposted to the famous beauty spot, Watersmeet, where the National Trust has an information bureau and—in summer—provides refreshments. You can continue to Lynmouth along a path by the river.

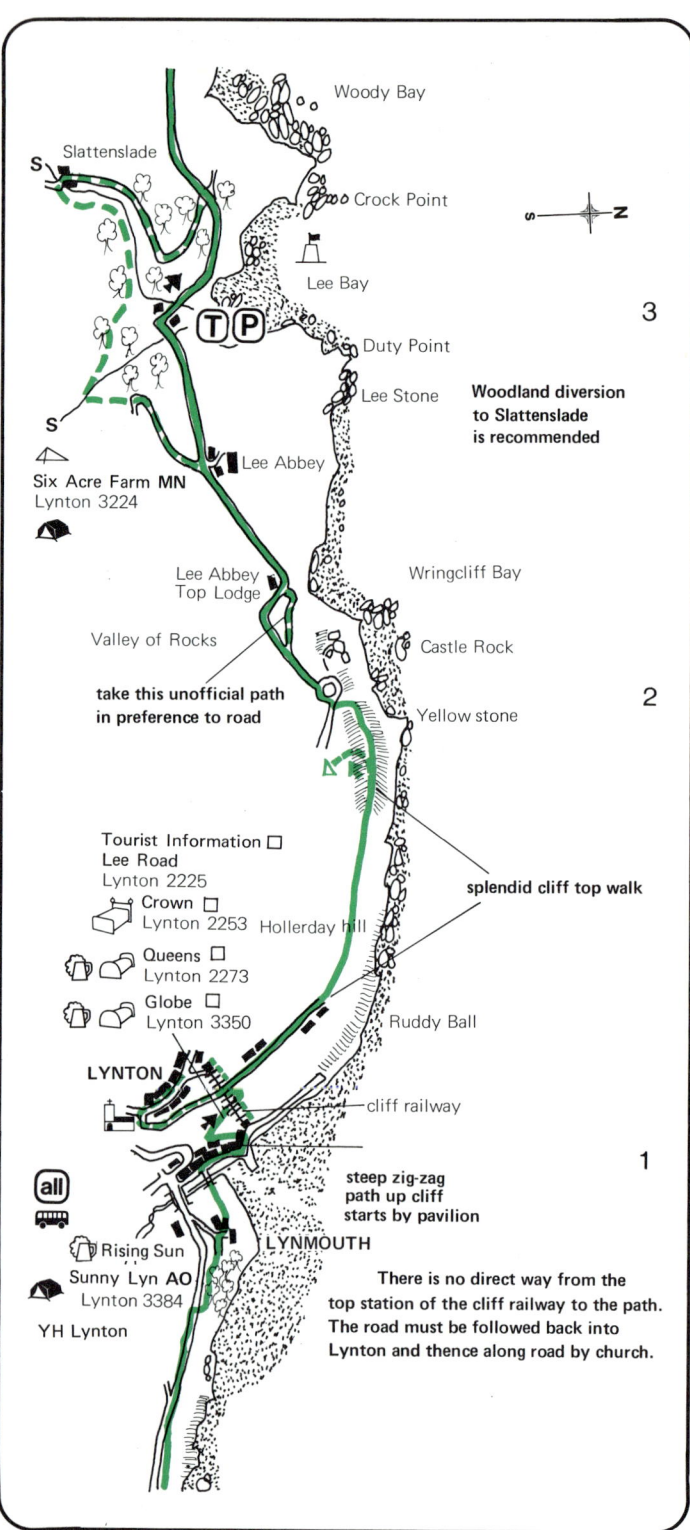

Woody Bay

Slattenslade

Crock Point

Lee Bay

Duty Point

T **P**

Lee Stone

**Woodland diversion
to Slattenslade
is recommended**

Six Acre Farm **MN**
Lynton 3224

Lee Abbey

Lee Abbey
Top Lodge

Wringcliff Bay

Valley of Rocks

Castle Rock

**take this unofficial path
in preference to road**

Yellow stone

Tourist Information □
Lee Road
Lynton 2225

Crown □
Lynton 2253

Hollerday hill

Queens □
Lynton 2273

Globe □
Lynton 3350

splendid cliff top walk

LYNTON

Ruddy Ball

cliff railway

all

**steep zig-zag
path up cliff
starts by pavilion**

Rising Sun

Sunny Lyn **AO**
Lynton 3384

LYNMOUTH

YH Lynton

There is no direct way from the
top station of the cliff railway to the path.
The road must be followed back into
Lynton and thence along road by church.

3

2

1

S ◆ N

6. Lynmouth Bay-Lynton-Woody Bay

3¾ miles 6km From Minehead 22¾ miles 37½km

Going: from Lynton there is the famous cliff walk to the Valley of the Rocks; from there on, a narrow coastal road of scenic beauty but a lot of cars in season.

Lynmouth, where the West Lyn and East Lyn rivers join before emptying into the sea, was a fishing village of varying fortunes over the centuries. Its popularity as a resort dates from the Napoleonic Wars when the Continent was barred to the gentry. Shelley (who brought his schoolgirl bride), Wordsworth, and Coleridge were among early visitors. There is a Youth Hostel. The town suffered in the flood disaster of August 1952 when 10in of rain fell in 24 hours. Hundreds of tons of boulders were brought down by the East Lyn river and did immense damage. Thirty-two people were killed.

High above Lynmouth is Lynton, a village converted by the Victorians into a resort. Thomas Coutts, the banker, and George Newnes, the publisher, did much to help in the development including the Cliff Railway, built in 1890. The tower of the church is 14th century, the rest 18–19th century. You can make the rewarding excursion on foot to Watersmeet (see section 5) by taking the footpath from the bridge running along the east bank of the East Lyn river.

The best means of reaching Lynton from Lynmouth is by the Cliff Railway which provides a frequent service in winter and summer. Then for the Coast Path follow the sign to the North Walk which starts on the narrow road, between the church and Valley of the Rocks Hotel. Alternatively, take the very steep zig-zag path up the cliff from the pavilion to North Walk. This leads to a level asphalted footpath, cut 150 years ago in the hillside 500ft up above the sea, with fine coastal views. The Path soon brings you to the Valley of the Rocks, with its rock pinnacles of fantastic shape, reminding one of a vast ruined castle which is, in fact, the name given to the most prominent pinnacle, Castle Rock. From the Valley of the Rocks join the narrow road to Lee Abbey and Woody Bay. *Lee Abbey is not an abbey—it is a Victorian mansion now used as a Church conference centre. If you wish to avoid a mile of road there is a woodland path signposted opposite the Abbey, taking you through woods before rejoining the road.*

By the toll gate cottage a path leads down to Lee Bay, with its grey sand and rocks. Refreshments at the cottage on summer weekdays.

The road winds up above Woody Bay through thick woods.

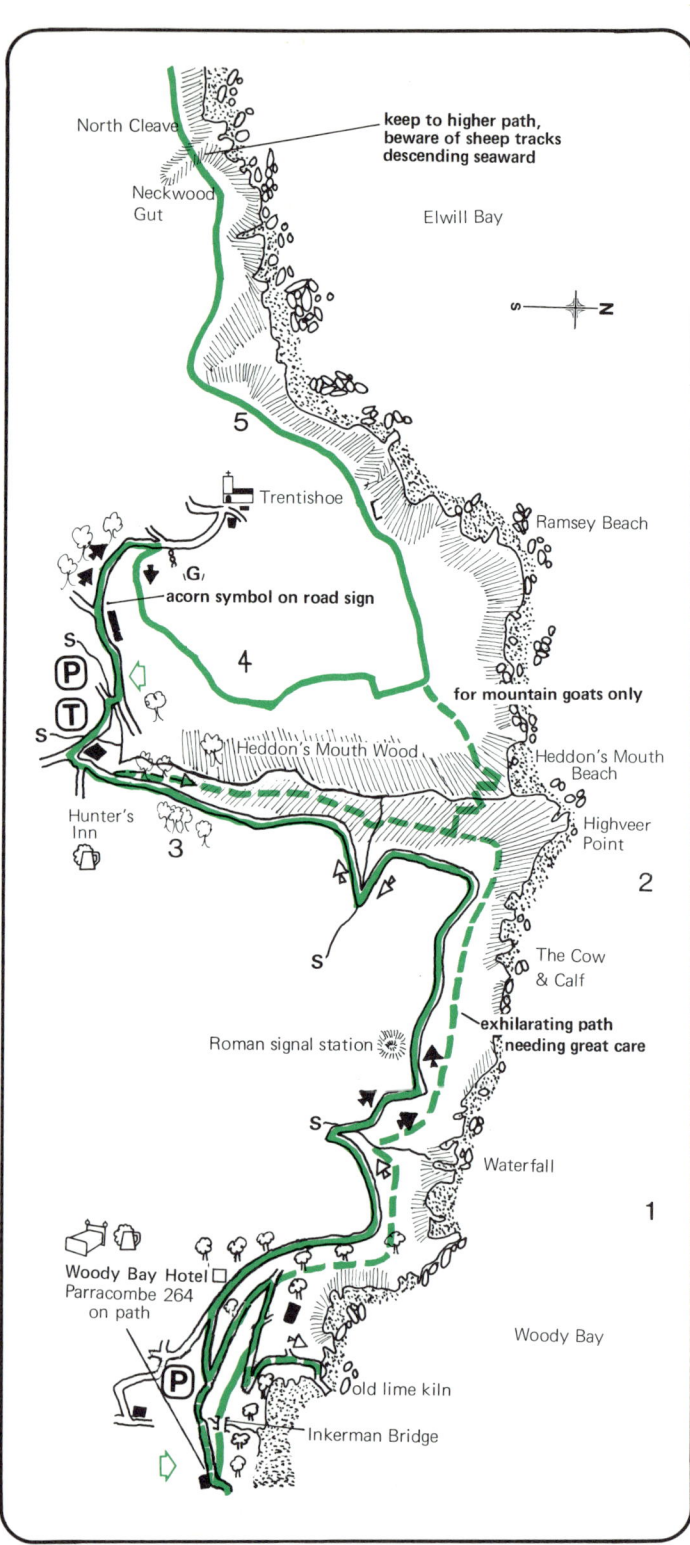

North Cleave

keep to higher path,
beware of sheep tracks
descending seaward

Neckwood
Gut

Elwill Bay

5

Trentishoe

G

acorn symbol on road sign

S

P

T

4

Ramsey Beach

S

for mountain goats only

Heddon's Mouth Wood

Heddon's Mouth
Beach

Hunter's
Inn

3

Highveer
Point

2

S

The Cow
& Calf

Roman signal station

exhilarating path
needing great care

S

Waterfall

1

Woody Bay Hotel
Parracombe 264
on path

P

old lime kiln

Inkerman Bridge

Woody Bay

7. Woody Bay-Heddon's Mouth-North Cleave

5¾ miles 9¼km   From Minehead 28½ miles 46¾km

Going: you have everything on this section—a short stretch of road, a fine grassy track along the cliff and inland to Hunter's Inn, a pull up to the other side of Heddon's Mouth, and another high cliff path with fine views from every angle. The going is from good to reasonable except for the last ¼ mile where the route is not very clear.

The official route continues along the road past Woody Bay Hotel.

A much recommended alternative is the attractive woodland path which goes down through the trees almost opposite the Hotel. When you join the road by a private garage you can turn right for a steep path down to Woody Bay Beach, or left to rejoin the official Path. A very exciting cliff walk goes off to the right at a sharp bend. Despite the danger warning signs this is a superb walk to Hunter's Inn for the sure-footed fell walker with a head for heights.

An attempt was made in the last century to develop Woody Bay as a resort. Beach of sand and rocks.

On the official route, past the Hotel and just beyond the National Trust car park, the Path leaves by a gate at a sharp bend.

You could not wish for a finer path than that starting from the gate: a wide level grassy track, at cliff-top height, at first through a grove of trees then out on the cliff with marvellous views wherever you look. You then come to the gorge of Heddon's Mouth Cleave with the scree-covered slope opposite dropping sheer to the Heddon's River below. On the high ground just inland of the Path, before you come to Heddon's Mouth Cleave, is the site of another Roman signal station of the 1st century similar to the one on Old Barrow (section 4). The Path turns inland along the Cleave entering woodland before arriving at Hunter's Inn, a pleasant refreshment stop. Keep your eyes open for ravens on the Path here.

You can if you wish walk along the river footpath to the beach at Heddon's Mouth—about ¾ hour for the return trip.

For the Coast Path keep on the road after crossing the bridge; ¼ mile down the road, past some cottages, there is a turning on the right with a sign to Trentishoe Common and Church. The Coast Path follows this route. Near to the top of the rise a footpath on the right leads up over a stretch of gorse-covered heath, the fringe of the Common. In a short while you are on the 600ft crest, looking down into Heddon's Mouth Cleave.

The Path becomes more of a sheep track running parallel with the line of the cliff, along the wire fence of the pastureland. After a broken stile the route seems to disappear: keep as high up the slope as possible and the path ahead will be seen.

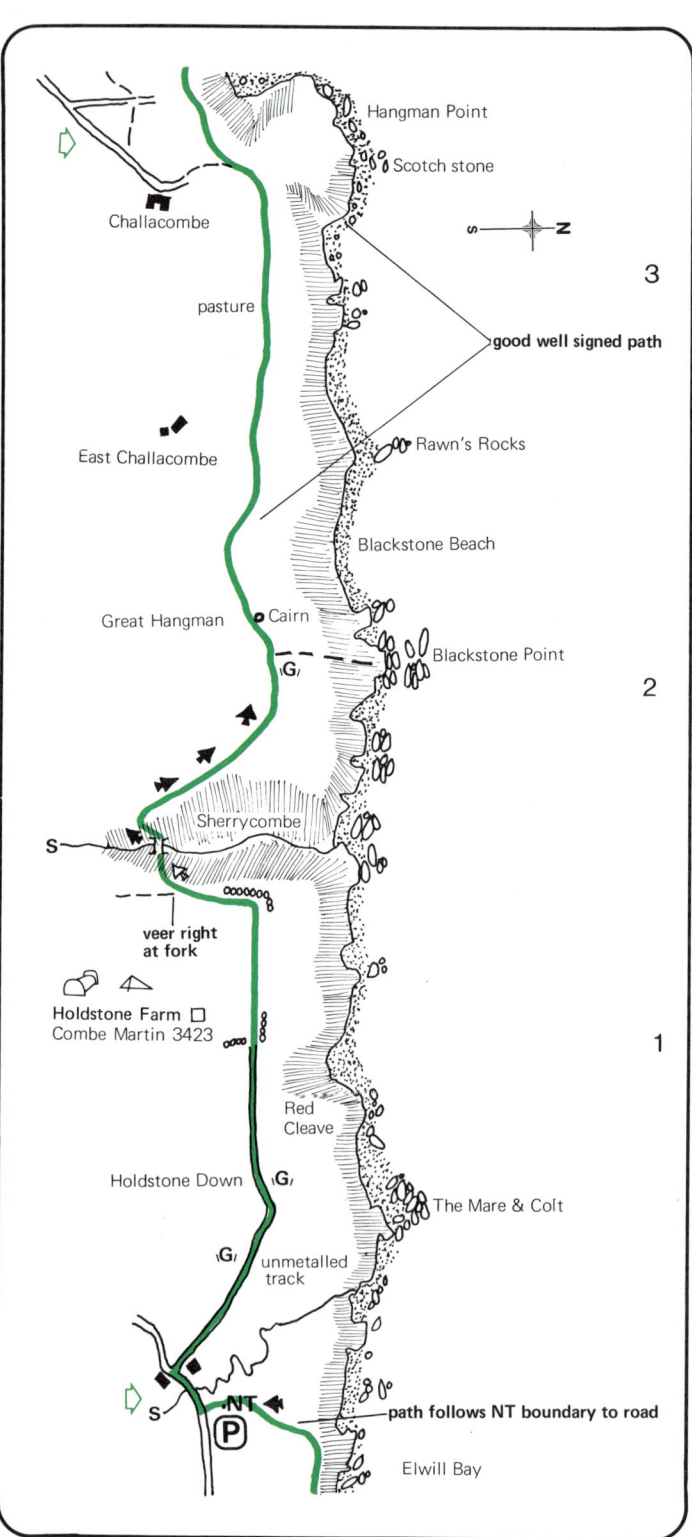

Hangman Point

Scotch stone

Challacombe

N

3

pasture

good well signed path

East Challacombe

Rawn's Rocks

Blackstone Beach

Great Hangman   Cairn

Blackstone Point

2

G

Sherrycombe

S

veer right
at fork

Holdstone Farm
Combe Martin 3423

Red
Cleave

1

Holdstone Down   G

The Mare & Colt

G   unmetalled
track

S   NT

path follows NT boundary to road

P

Elwill Bay

8. Elwill Bay-Blackstone Point-Hangman Point

3½ miles 5½km   From Minehead 32 miles 51¼km

Going: over moorland, high above the sea, with a long climb up the Great Hangman. The going is good, especially the start of the descent to Combe Martin, and well signposted throughout.

At North Cleave (previous map), as you come across the moorland, a Coast Path sign directs you up a track inland which brings you shortly to the road between Hunter's Inn and Combe Martin and a few cottages. This is the west boundary of National Trust territory. Past the cottages the Coast Path continues as a wide track leading seaward over moor. Ahead of you looms the huge bulk of the 1044ft Great Hangman, looking sinister in any light but the brightest. Soon the moorland track turns inland round Headstone Hill (1145ft) to negotiate Sherrycombe, the valley you have to cross before tackling the Great Hangman.

The Path makes its way easily down the hillside to the rather muddy approach to the footbridge crossing the stream. On the other side the Path climbs the slope, its zig-zag reducing as much as possible the effort needed. The cairn on the summit of the Great Hangman is eventually reached, with magnificent views—ahead of you to Combe Martin and, beyond, to Widmouth Head and the indentation of Water Mouth; behind you, if clear, the cliffs above Heddon's Mouth, Foreland Point, and the Welsh coast the other side of the Bristol Channel.

Note the hump-back nature of the cliffs on this part of the coast where the rounded though very steep slopes, covered with grass or other vegetation reach down almost to the sea. This is in contrast to the cliff scene farther down the coast: at Land's End, for example, where the cliffs drop sheer to the sea as though sliced with a gigantic knife. This is mainly due to the vertical jointing of the rocks. Great slabs are removed by the under-cutting action of strong seas.

Just before the crest of Great Hangman a path leads to Blackstone Point, another good viewpoint.

From the top of Great Hangman a pleasant cliff path leads down towards Combe Martin, passing the base of the Little Hangman Hill.

You can divert off the Coast Path down to the little Wild Pear beach (section 9), of rock and grey sand.

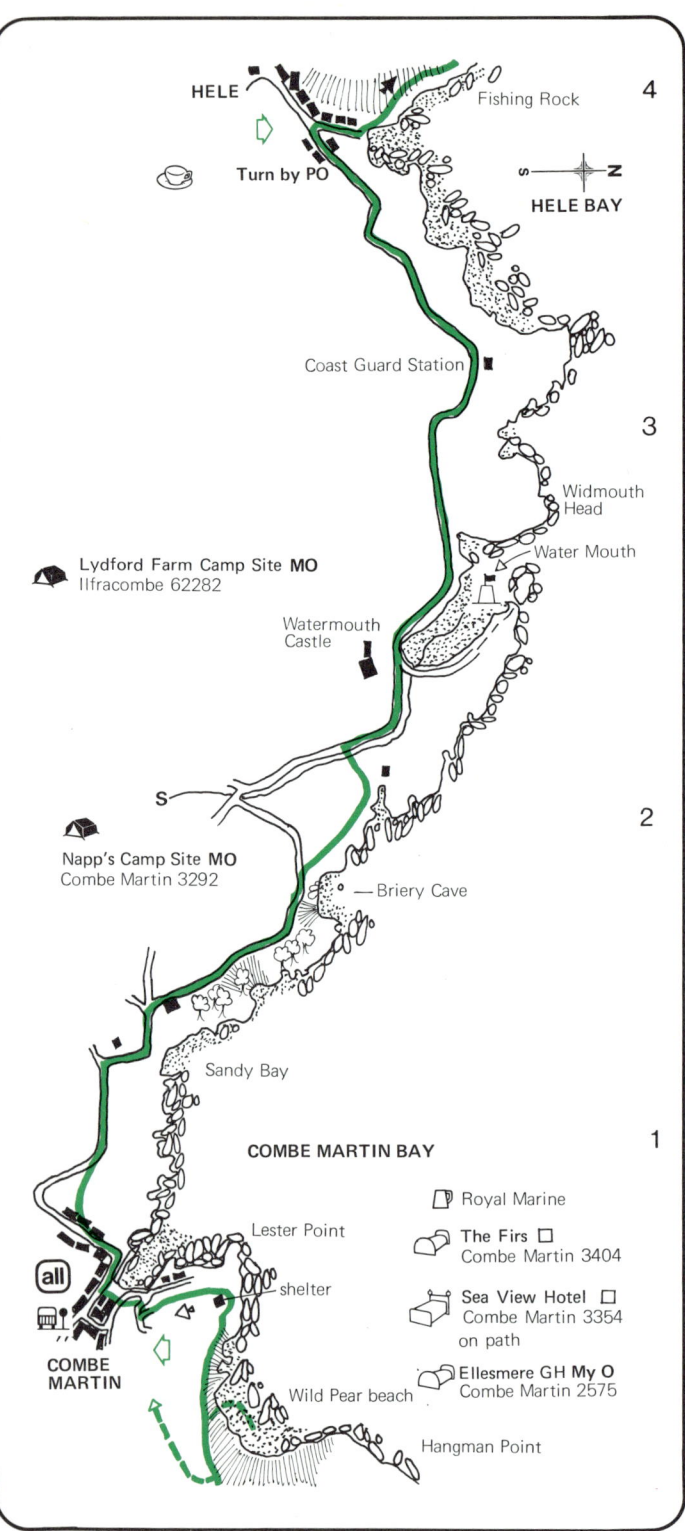

HELE

Fishing Rock

4

Turn by PO

HELE BAY

S ✦ N

Coast Guard Station

3

Widmouth Head

Water Mouth

Lydford Farm Camp Site **MO**
Ilfracombe 62282

Watermouth Castle

Napp's Camp Site **MO**
Combe Martin 3292

S

2

Briery Cave

Sandy Bay

COMBE MARTIN BAY

1

Royal Marine

Lester Point

The Firs ☐
Combe Martin 3404

shelter

Sea View Hotel ☐
Combe Martin 3354
on path

COMBE MARTIN

Ellesmere GH **My O**
Combe Martin 2575

Wild Pear beach

Hangman Point

9. Hangman Point-Combe Martin-Hele Bay

4 miles 6½km   From Minehead 36 miles 58km

Going: good path for the short distance down to Combe Martin, from then on not at all satisfactory, involving walking along the main road for most of the way. You would not miss much if you took the bus from Combe Martin to Hele Bay or Ilfracombe.

After rounding the Little Hangman and passing above Wild Pear Beach the narrow Path brings you into the 'Hangman Path' leading along the edge of the large car park near the front in Combe Martin.

You have now arrived at the west boundary of the Exmoor National Park; there is an Exmoor National Park kiosk in the car park during the summer. The Park authorities have done a fine signposting job on their 36-mile section of the Coast Path.

Combe Martin is a small resort which straggles down the main road inland for over 1 mile. Sandy Bay has as much of rocks as of sand. The handsome church at the landward end of the village has a remarkably high tower.

Leaving Combe Martin a Coast Path sign shows the way down a narrow lane, past some old cottages, cutting off a corner of the main road. After that you have to walk along this main road until the Sandy Bay Hotel at the side of which a wide track, with a footpath sign, leads through woods for ½ mile.

On this Path is the Napps Camp site.

You are brought back to the busy main road: more road walking, past the Water Mouth inlet with its caravan site and boats, until after another mile you dip down to Hele Bay. Here, from the small quay (refreshment café) you regain the Coast Path which climbs up and around the 447ft Hillsborough hill.

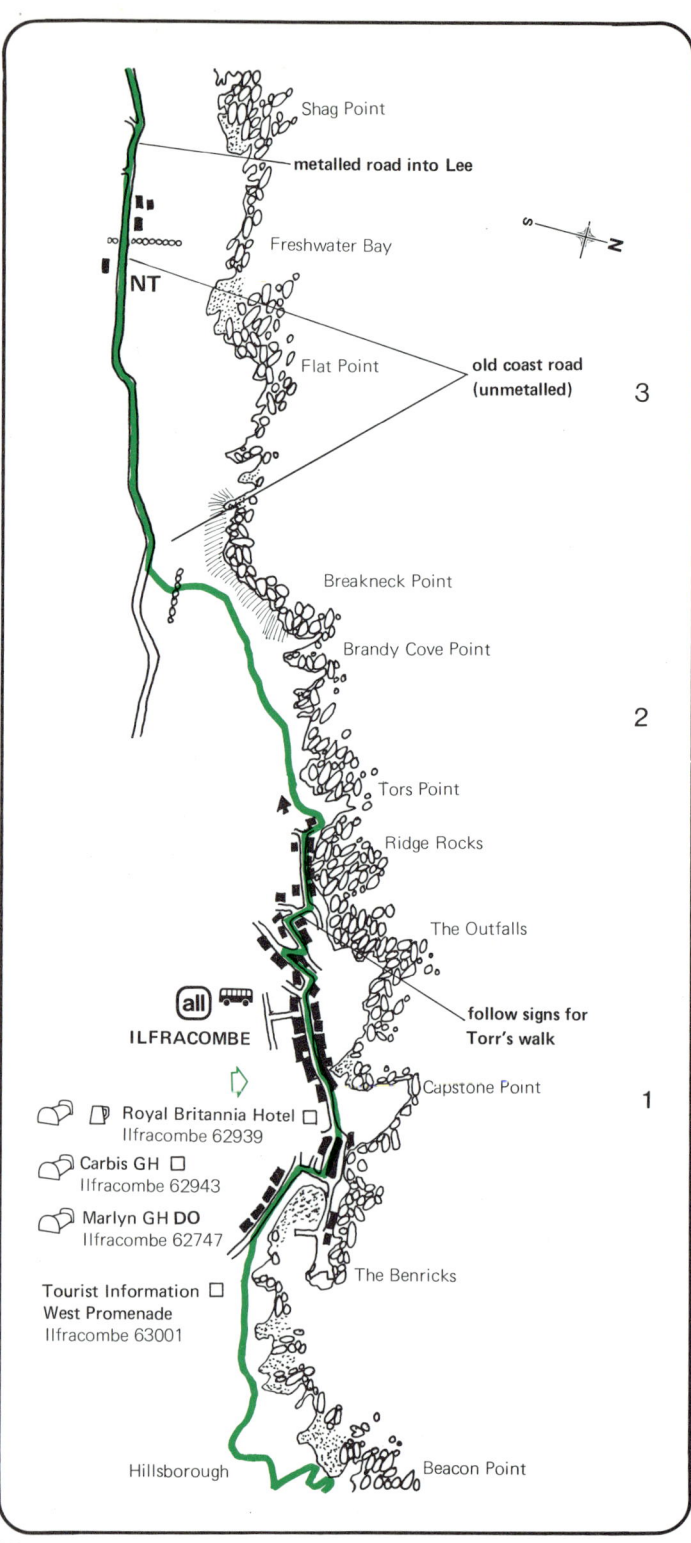

metalled road into Lee

Shag Point

Freshwater Bay

NT

Flat Point

old coast road
(unmetalled)

3

Breakneck Point

Brandy Cove Point

2

Tors Point

Ridge Rocks

The Outfalls

all 🚌

ILFRACOMBE

follow signs for
Torr's walk

Capstone Point

1

Royal Britannia Hotel ☐
Ilfracombe 62939

Carbis GH ☐
Ilfracombe 62943

Marlyn GH DO
Ilfracombe 62747

The Benricks

Tourist Information ☐
West Promenade
Ilfracombe 63001

Hillsborough

Beacon Point

10. Hele Bay-Ilfracombe-Shag Point
3¾ miles 6km From Minehead 39¾ miles 64km

Going: this section contains two good easy stretches of cliff-walking each side of Ilfracombe.

From Hele Bay the Coast Path zig-zags up Hillsborough hill (447ft) bringing you over the top and down the other side where it runs close to the edge of the cliff.

In the spring and early summer you have a very close view of nesting herring gulls, fulmars, and kittiwakes.

As you come over the top of Hillsborough a fine panorama of Ilfracombe with its harbour and prominent Lantern Hill. The Path brings you out through pleasure gardens to the Harbour, usually full of sailing craft and a small coaster or two, passing above two beaches: Larkstone Beach and Rapparee Cove, with rocks and grey sand.

Ilfracombe (pop 8900) has been a fishing port of some importance since the Middle Ages. Granted a charter by Edward I in 1278 it was regularly called upon to provide ships and men in times of war. Holy Trinity church is 15th century with earlier parts, and the Chapel of St Nicholas on Lantern Hill, probably 14th century, recently restored. Of the number of pubs the oldest is undoubtedly the George and Dragon, dating from 1360. It was renovated in 1641!

Ilfracombe started to become a popular resort early in the last century and is now the largest on the north Devon coast. From its harbour a steamer runs trips in the summer to the Welsh coast and the island of Lundy, both of which can be seen on a clear day.

The Coast Path west of Ilfracombe starts on Torr's Walk, reached by Osborne Road which runs east of Holy Trinity church. Keep climbing until you come out on the cliff high above the town. The very good Path then continues along the side of the 400ft cliff with more close views of breeding gulls, also stonechats, whitethroats, and other birds fond of gorse and bramble. You eventually come out on an open stretch of turf where a stile and a sign indicates the start of the National Trust Flat Point, a fine open cliff-top area. From Shag Point, along the route, there is a good view ahead of Bull Point, of characteristic shape.

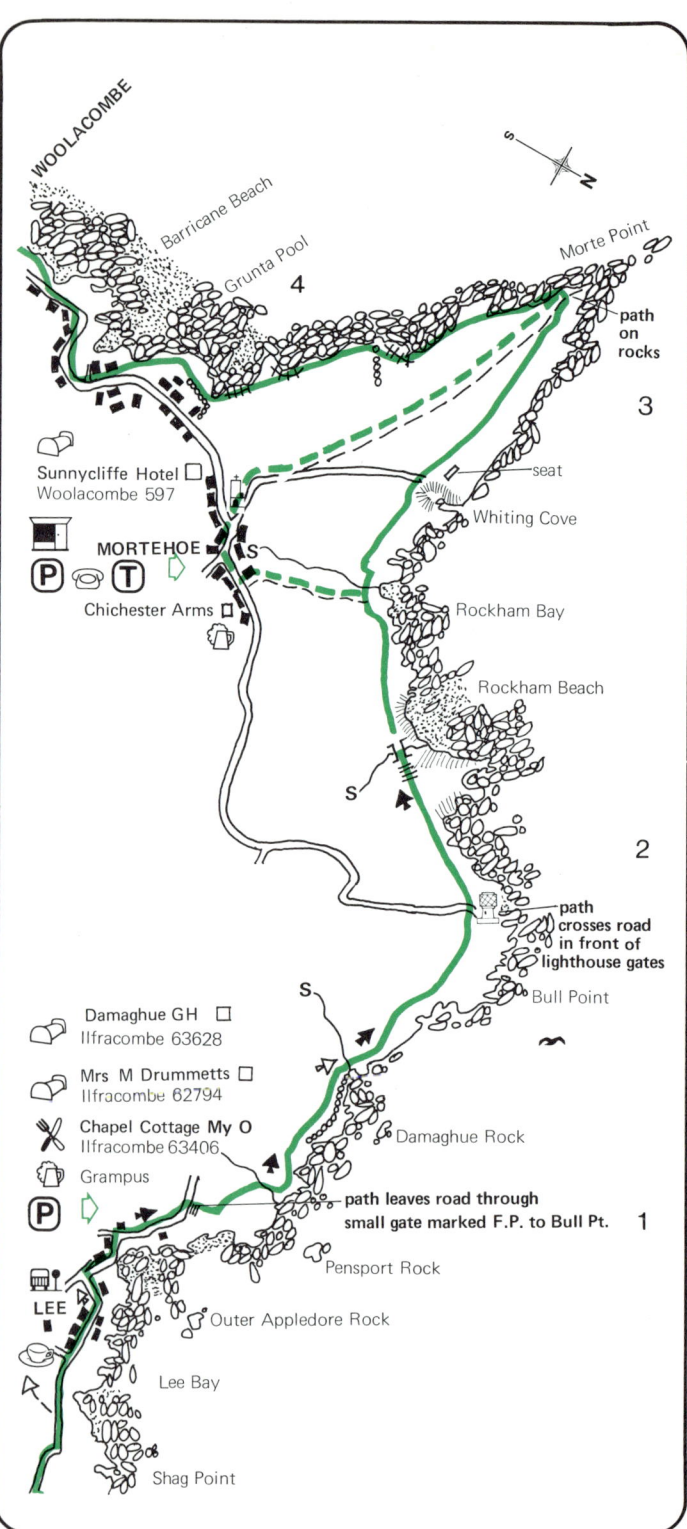

WOOLACOMBE

Barricane Beach

Grunta Pool

4

Morte Point

path on rocks

3

Sunnycliffe Hotel □
Woolacombe 597

seat

Whiting Cove

MORTEHOE S

P ☕ T

Chichester Arms □

Rockham Bay

Rockham Beach

S

2

path crosses road in front of lighthouse gates

Bull Point

Damaghue GH □
Ilfracombe 63628

Mrs M Drummetts □
Ilfracombe 62794

S

Chapel Cottage My O
Ilfracombe 63406

Grampus

P

Damaghue Rock

path leaves road through
small gate marked F.P. to Bull Pt.

1

LEE

Pensport Rock

Outer Appledore Rock

Lee Bay

Shag Point

11. Shag Point-Lee-Woolacombe

4¾ miles 7¾km   From Minehead 44½ miles 71¾km

Going: a fine well walked cliff path.

At the gate which is the west boundary of the National Trust's Flat Point you come to a narrow country lane running steeply down to Lee Bay, between high hedges.

As you walk down to the Bay you have a fine view of the valley. On both sides are thick woods among which are large clumps of purple rhododendrons which in early summer, with the varying shades of green of the trees, make an unforgettable picture. On the left of the country lane is a footpath leading over the fields to the village of Lee with thatched cottages and an old pub, The Grampus.

The lane joins the road down to the Bay coming out at the side of the large Lee Bay Hotel. There are rare ducks and multi-horned rams at the delightful Chapel Cottage restaurant.

From the beach take the road climbing up on the west side. After ¼ mile a gate will be seen on the right opening on the National Trust Damage Cliff property and the Coast Path to Bull Point. The going is good, with two small combes on route, and the Path eventually crosses the metalled track leading to the Bull Point lighthouse (visits on weekday afternoons). Following the signs you then drop down to Rockham Bay, with good sands.

¼ mile inland by footpath from here is the village of Mortehoe (pub).

The Path continues above Rockham Bay along a narrow rocky track following closely the coastline, at times not very high above the frequently turbulent sea, bringing you to Morte Point where the rocks taper off into the sea in menacing reefs. The swirling waters of the tidal race extending way beyond the Point add to the intimidating scene.

Many ships were wrecked here in the days of sail, one tragedy being that of a naval vessel which was lost here in a gale in 1799, her captain and crew, 105 in all, being drowned.
Turning the Point the Path takes you east along the other side until you come to the outskirts of Woolacombe and the road down to the Bay.

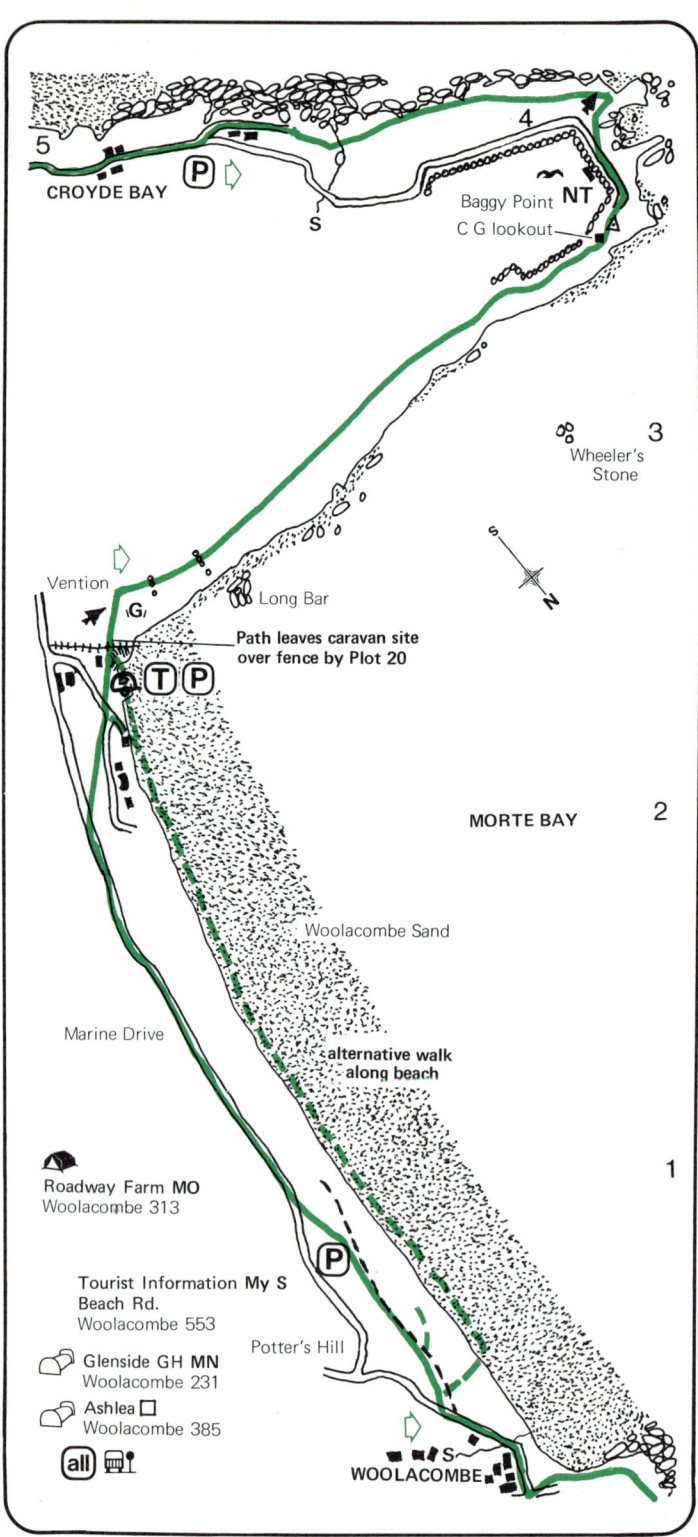

5 CROYDE BAY

4

Baggy Point **NT**
C G lookout

3

Wheeler's
Stone

Vention

Long Bar

Path leaves caravan site
over fence by Plot 20

MORTE BAY 2

Woolacombe Sand

Marine Drive

alternative walk
along beach

1

Roadway Farm **MO**
Woolacombe 313

Tourist Information My S
Beach Rd.
Woolacombe 553

Glenside GH **MN**
Woolacombe 231

Ashlea □
Woolacombe 385

Potter's Hill

WOOLACOMBE

12. Woolacombe-Baggy Point-Croyde Bay
5 miles 8km   From Minehead 49½ miles 79¾km

Going: quite a change—a long walk through sand dunes or along sands and then a high cliff walk, mostly on field path.

After turning Morte Point (section 11) you have had for some time a view of Woolacombe and its 2-mile-wide magnificent sandy bay.

Here, because of a change in the rock formation, the sands are yellow in contrast to the grey sand beaches we have previously encountered. Surfing is popular but bathing would be dangerous.

The 'centre' of Woolacombe is round the corner of the road. There is a large licensed café catering for the large numbers flocking to Woolacombe in the season. Along the road going south parallel to the coast, a bridle-way on the right takes the Coast Path for some distance through the dunes (known as Woolacombe Warren), but seems to peter out after about 1 mile. You can take to the sands if you wish.

The exit from the far end of Woolacombe Sand (as the beach is called) leads up past the large house, Vention. This comes out on a metalled road with a large car park on the right. Cross the car park and in the far corner of the caravan site, a field path starts to climb towards the crest of the ridge in front of you: the Coast Path follows this along the crest by a well-marked level track at the side of pasture and arable farmland.

This is more National Trust land; at the apparently disused Coast Guard Lookout the Path makes a turn along a stone wall round Baggy Point.

In the early summer this wall is covered with pink thrift and white stonecrop providing a display which rivals any garden rockery. Baggy Point is one of the spots on this coast for observing migrating birds: shearwaters, gannets, finches, larks, etc, leaving the country in the autumn. Herring gulls, fulmars, kittiwakes and the occasional raven nest on the cliffs.

On the Point there is a wide farm track leading east along the other side of the headland but the official Path drops down the slope, giving a better view of the rocky edge, all the way into Croyde Bay.

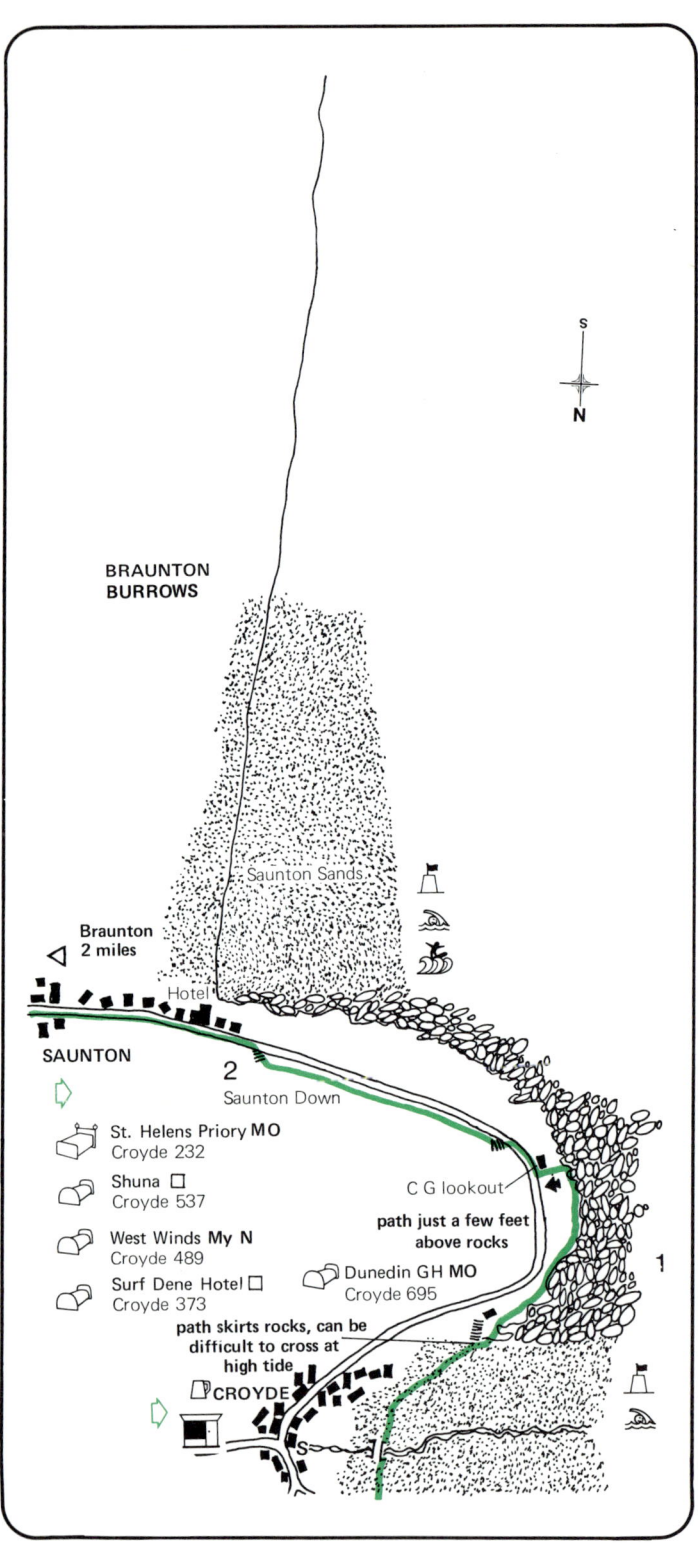

BRAUNTON
BURROWS

Saunton Sands

Braunton
2 miles

Hotel

SAUNTON

2
Saunton Down

St. Helens Priory **MO**
Croyde 232

Shuna ☐
Croyde 537

West Winds **My N**
Croyde 489

Surf Dene Hotel ☐
Croyde 373

Dunedin GH **MO**
Croyde 695

C G lookout

**path just a few feet
above rocks**

**path skirts rocks, can be
difficult to cross at
high tide**

CROYDE

S

1

S
N

13. Croyde Bay-Saunton

3 miles 4¾km   From Minehead 52½ miles 84½km

Going: not an attractive section—most of the Path is only a few feet above the main road.

Unless you need something to eat or drink there is no need to go 1 mile inland to the village of Croyde. You can walk across the sandy beach where, on the far side, a path leads off the sands and continues as a winding narrow track along the edge of the low sandstone cliff, above jagged rocks. This leads eventually out on the main road where, after a few yards, the Path continues, running a few feet above the road on the landward side then, after 1 mile, back on the road again, opposite a large hotel at Saunton. Here the Coast Path comes to a temporary end.

From Saunton you can see Braunton Burrows, a large area of sand dunes stretching south for 4 miles, 1 mile wide, and rising to 100ft in the centre. It is composed of a mixture of rock and shell sand and is of great interest to naturalists. The southernmost tip is a Nature Reserve with a Nature Trail (for information ring Braunton 552). In the hollows there are pools, and here and elsewhere there is a variety of plants and wildflowers including such rarities as the water germander. The Burrows are a favourite stop-over for migrant birds, particularly in the autumn and, among others, wheaters breed there. There is a firing range on the Burrows; a red flag indicates prohibited areas during firing.

Saunton-Hartland Point

From Saunton to Hartland Point, nearly 25 miles westward along the coast, there is no continuous Coast Path. Negotiations are in hand but at the time of writing only short isolated stretches of Path are available. Here are the sections concerned.
From Westward Ho!, westward: about 3 miles.
Eastward and westward of Bucks Mills: about 1 mile.
Hobby Drive from the A39 (MR 336234) to Clovelly: 3 miles.
Clovelly westward—Mouth Mill: 3 miles.

There is no alternative path or any public transport to connect Mouth Mill with Hartland Point where the Path restarts.
There is a bus service between Saunton and Barnstaple and between Barnstaple and the village of Hartland. From Hartland to Hartland Point is a 3½-mile walk along a country lane. Alternatively, you can make for Hartland Quay (3 miles south of Hartland Point) 2 miles west of Hartland.

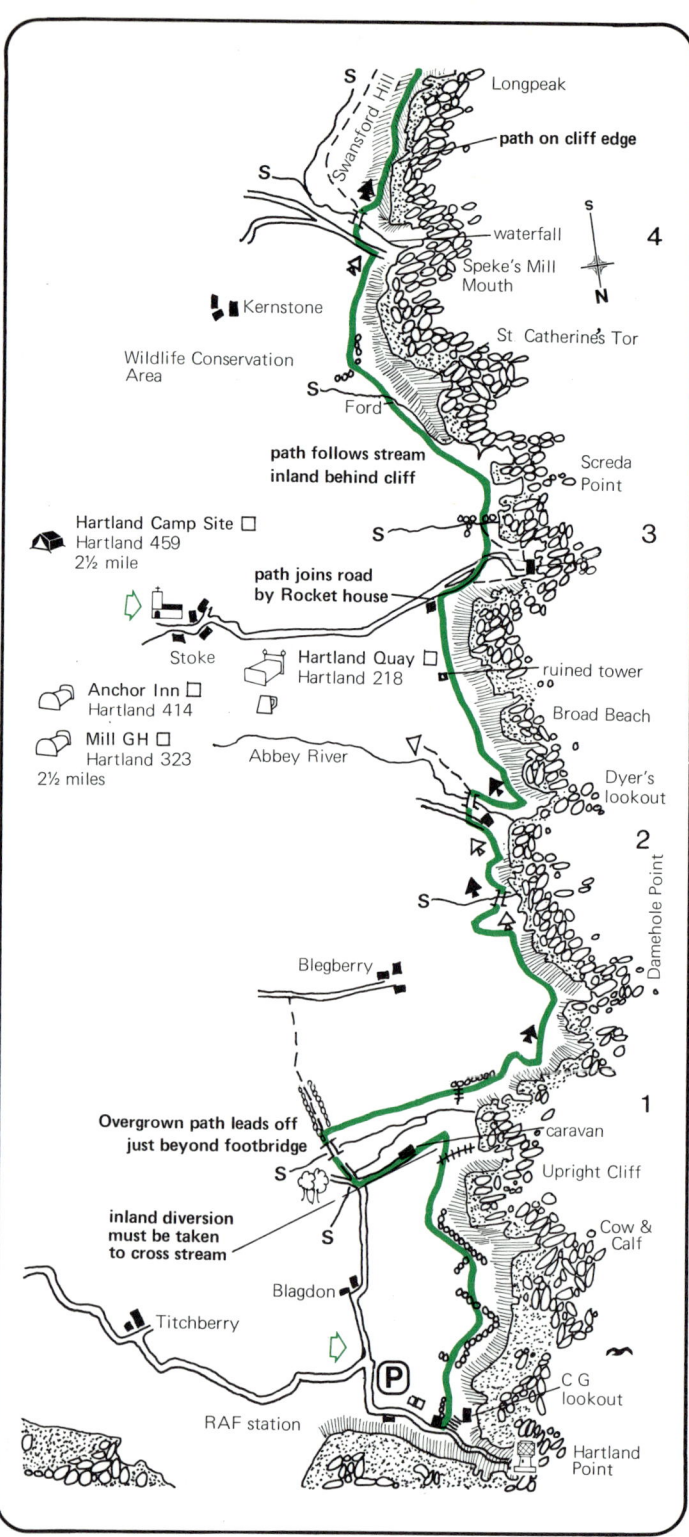

S

Longpeak

path on cliff edge

Swansford Hill

S

waterfall

Speke's Mill Mouth

Kernstone

St Catherine's Tor

Wildlife Conservation Area

S

Ford

Screda Point

path follows stream inland behind cliff

S

Hartland Camp Site ☐
Hartland 459
2½ mile

path joins road by Rocket house

Stoke

Hartland Quay ☐
Hartland 218

ruined tower

Anchor Inn ☐
Hartland 414

Broad Beach

Mill GH ☐
Hartland 323
2½ miles

Abbey River

Dyer's lookout

2

Damehole Point

S

Blegberry

Overgrown path leads off just beyond footbridge

caravan

S

Upright Cliff

inland diversion must be taken to cross stream

S

Cow & Calf

Blagdon

Titchberry

C G lookout

P

RAF station

Hartland Point

14. Hartland Point-Longpeak

4½ miles 7¼km   From Minehead 57 miles* 91¾km*

Going: three steep combes to be negotiated on this section, but spectacular scenes of rock and sea. If clear you should be able to see the island of Lundy about 12 miles north of Hartland Point.

Unless you have been lucky in getting a lift you will have to reach Hartland Point on foot as there is no public transport. The Point is 3½ miles by country road from Hartland which has a bus service.

The Coast Path starts by the white gate leading to the Hartland Point Lighthouse from the car park. The lighthouse can be visited on weekly afternoons. The Path is at first well signposted and runs below the Coast Guard Lookout keeping to the seaward edge of arable and pasture land. You soon reach the heights above the first combe, shown on the map as Upright Cliff. After dropping down to the bottom of the valley you must take the farm track leading inland for almost ½ mile before crossing the stream by a bridge (there is an unauthorised crossing nearer the sea, close to a caravan which stands on its own in a field).

From the stream the Path climbs up the ridge and runs along the crest towards the sea turning south above the spectacular Damehole Point. Almost immediately there is another combe with steep sides, after which you come to the valley of the Abbey River.

Abbey River flows past the site of Hartland Abbey 1½ miles upstream. On the height of the valley opposite is a ruined lookout tower, built to watch for Barbary pirates. Looking inland the 15th-century tower of Stoke church can be seen.

There is a very overgrown path dropping down diagonally through the gorse to the floor of the Abbey River valley; better to keep to the steep path at the edge of the cliff, but watch your step.

The Path continues over heathland past the tower and comes out at the Toll Bar on the road down to Hartland Quay where there is an hotel (refreshments) and swimming pool. A wide track then takes the path to pass inland round the 280ft St Catherine's Tor, across another stream and a field, up over a rise and down to Speke's Mill Mouth with its waterfall, delightful valley, and beach.

The area is one of 'special scientific interest' for its range of flowers.

The ascent from here is not quite so steep as the others on this section, and you emerge on an upland of fine unspoiled country.

**not including Saunton-Hartland Point*

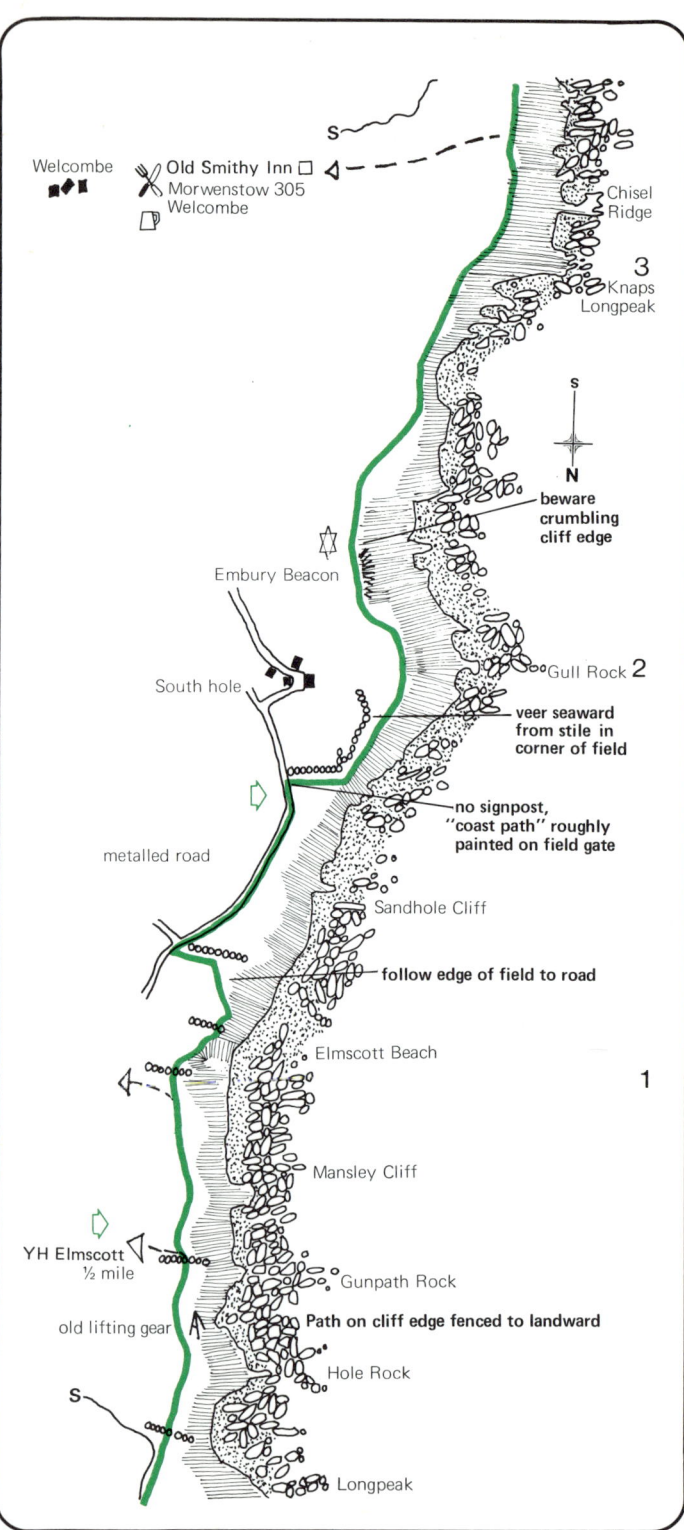

Welcome

Old Smithy Inn
Morwenstow 305
Welcombe

Chisel
Ridge

3
Knaps
Longpeak

S
N

beware
crumbling
cliff edge

Embury Beacon

Gull Rock **2**

South hole

veer seaward
from stile in
corner of field

no signpost,
"coast path" roughly
painted on field gate

metalled road

Sandhole Cliff

follow edge of field to road

Elmscott Beach

1

Mansley Cliff

YH Elmscott
½ mile

Gunpath Rock

old lifting gear

Path on cliff edge fenced to landward

Hole Rock

S

Longpeak

15. Longpeak-Chisel Ridge
3½ miles 5½km From Minehead 60½ miles 97½km

Going: a fine stretch of level cliff-top walking, with a short distance on the road.

From Speke's Mill Mouth (section 14) the Coast Path climbs up over the turf and then along a narrow track, to the top of the cliff. From here the Path runs on an even and level course along the cliff keeping to the seaward side of hayfields and sheep pasture.

Along this section, when you are not preoccupied with climbing or descending steep slopes, you have a chance of observing the abundance and variety of wild flowers, butterflies and birds, all typical of this 16-mile stretch of coast from Hartland to Bude. In early summer masses of pale pink thrift contrast with the yellow of the gorse and birdsfoot trefoil, the red campion, foxgloves and, in damp spots, yellow iris. Butterflies likely to be seen include the meadow brown, common blue, the wall butterfly, and occasional peacock. Watch out for a buzzard hunting above the cliffs and the kestrel. On the heath, you can see and hear stonechats, usually in pairs, and whitethroat.

The derricks and lifting gear, now derelict and rusty, on the cliff-top, were to haul salvage up the 400ft cliff from the 3500-ton RFA tanker Green Ranger *which was blown on the rocks in a November gale in 1962 while being towed to Cardiff. Her seven-man crew were rescued with difficulty by breeches buoy.*

After just over 1 mile a signpost directs you inland for a short distance to the road. You have 5–10 minutes walk along this road to the point where the Path gets back to the cliff. The road is not a busy one.

Half a mile up the road to the north-east from where you first joined it is the Elmscott Youth Hostel which can also be reached by footpath from the Coast Path.

The Path continues along the cliff-top over rough pasture. Close to the edge of the cliff the route lies through the gorse-covered Embury Beacon.

On Embury Beacon are the clear traces of a cliff-fort with widely-spaced ramparts, reckoned to be Iron Age. Cliff falls have eaten into the site.

Another ¾ mile and you come out high above the Welcombe Mouth valley at Chisel Ridge. A rough track from Welcombe village allows cars to the car park by the small rocky beach.

1½ miles inland is a pub, the Old Smithy. In the summer you can buy stores at the farm nearby.

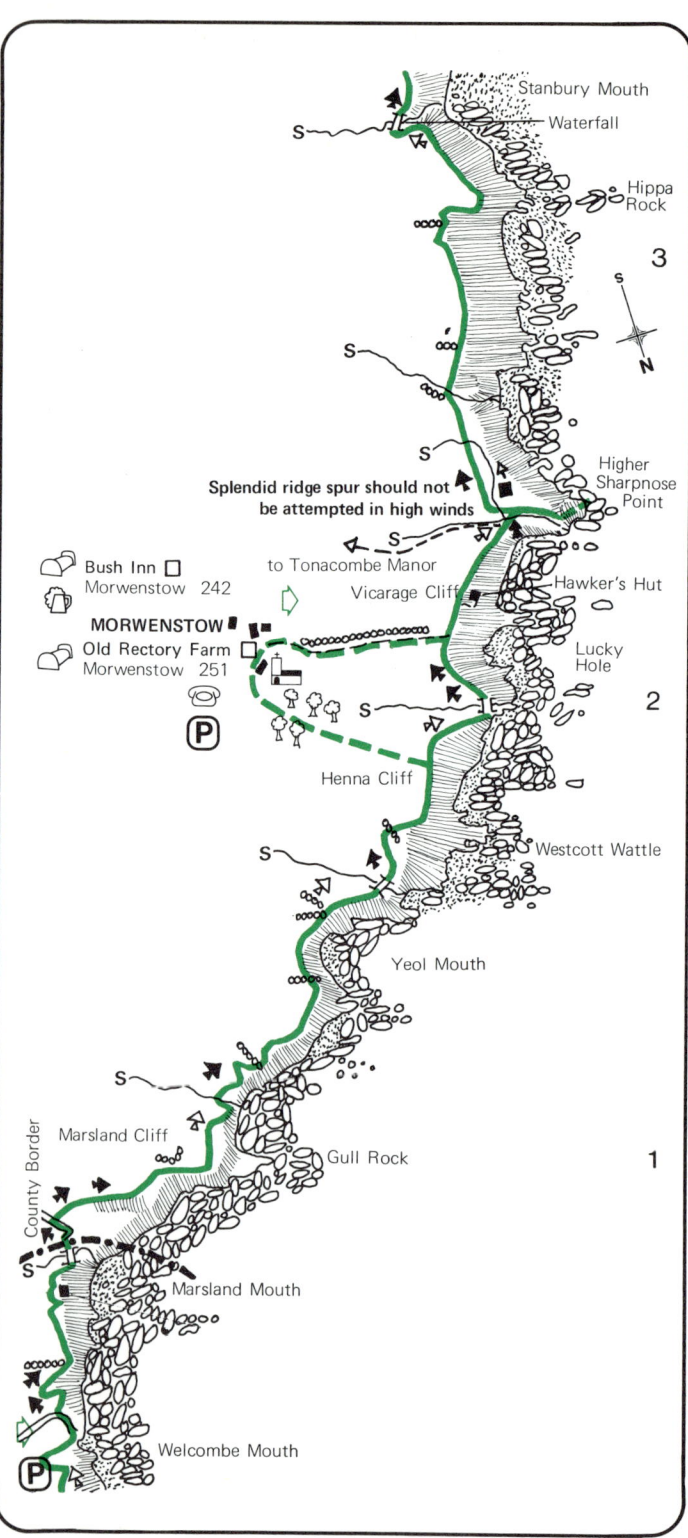

Stanbury Mouth

Waterfall

Hippa Rock

3

Higher Sharpnose Point

Splendid ridge spur should not be attempted in high winds

Hawker's Hut

to Tonacombe Manor

Vicarage Cliff

Bush Inn
Morwenstow 242

MORWENSTOW

Old Rectory Farm
Morwenstow 251

P

Lucky Hole

2

Henna Cliff

Westcott Wattle

Yeol Mouth

Marsland Cliff

Gull Rock

1

County Border

Marsland Mouth

Welcombe Mouth

P

16. Welcombe Mouth-Marsland Mouth-Stanbury Mouth

3¾ miles 6km From Minehead 64¼ miles 103½km

Going: between Welcombe Mouth and Stanbury Mouth you have no less than five steep-sided combes to cross which makes this section hard work and not to be attempted by elderly or inexperienced walkers. If you can manage it the effort is very worthwhile, with stupendous cliff and ocean scenery.

The Path rises steeply out of Welcombe Mouth and, once on the top and across a field, drops just as steeply down to the pleasant stream which is the boundary between Devon and Cornwall, passing a small hut which must provide its owner with a magnificent observation post. Cross the footbridge and you should find the start of the North Cornwall Coast Path, adequately signposted, zig-zagging up the hillside. At first the Path goes round the hill before climbing to the top inside a barbed wire fence.

Note the twisted strata of Gull Rock just off the coast.

From the top of Marsland Cliff, the Path goes almost straight down to another deep little combe and out again. Along Cornakey Cliff you come to another combe with a small waterfall. Then up to Henna Cliff, the Path emerges above a wider valley. Looking inland you can see, up the valley and surrounded by trees, the church and village of Morwenstow. A short way down the slope a footpath turns inland from the Coast Path which brings you (½ mile) to the woods and the vicarage. This was the home of the Cornish poet and eccentric parson, the Reverend R S Hawker (1803–75). *The chimneys of the vicarage are said to represent the church towers of the parishes where he was before he came to Morwenstow. His best known work was* The Song of the Western Men *and he is reputed to have introduced the Harvest Festival Service. Always keen on the moral welfare of his flock he dealt severely with any who helped themselves to 'salvage' from the many wrecks on this dangerous coast—many victims of which were buried in his churchyard. He was also energetic in attempts to save the lives of the unfortunate crews. Village pubs: the Bush.*

You can regain the Coast Path by the footpath from the church up the south slope of the valley. Continuing along the Path you come to a National Trust 'Hawker's Hut' sign and a few yards down the cliff is the hut, built by Hawker himself out of driftwood where he could write in solitude. The next valley is of the river Tidna.

One mile inland is the 16th-century manor of Tonacombe, with secret chambers.

Coming out above Stanbury Mouth the scene ahead is dominated by the huge tracking station on the hill on the other side of the valley. The Path down to the stream runs close to the edge of the cliff.

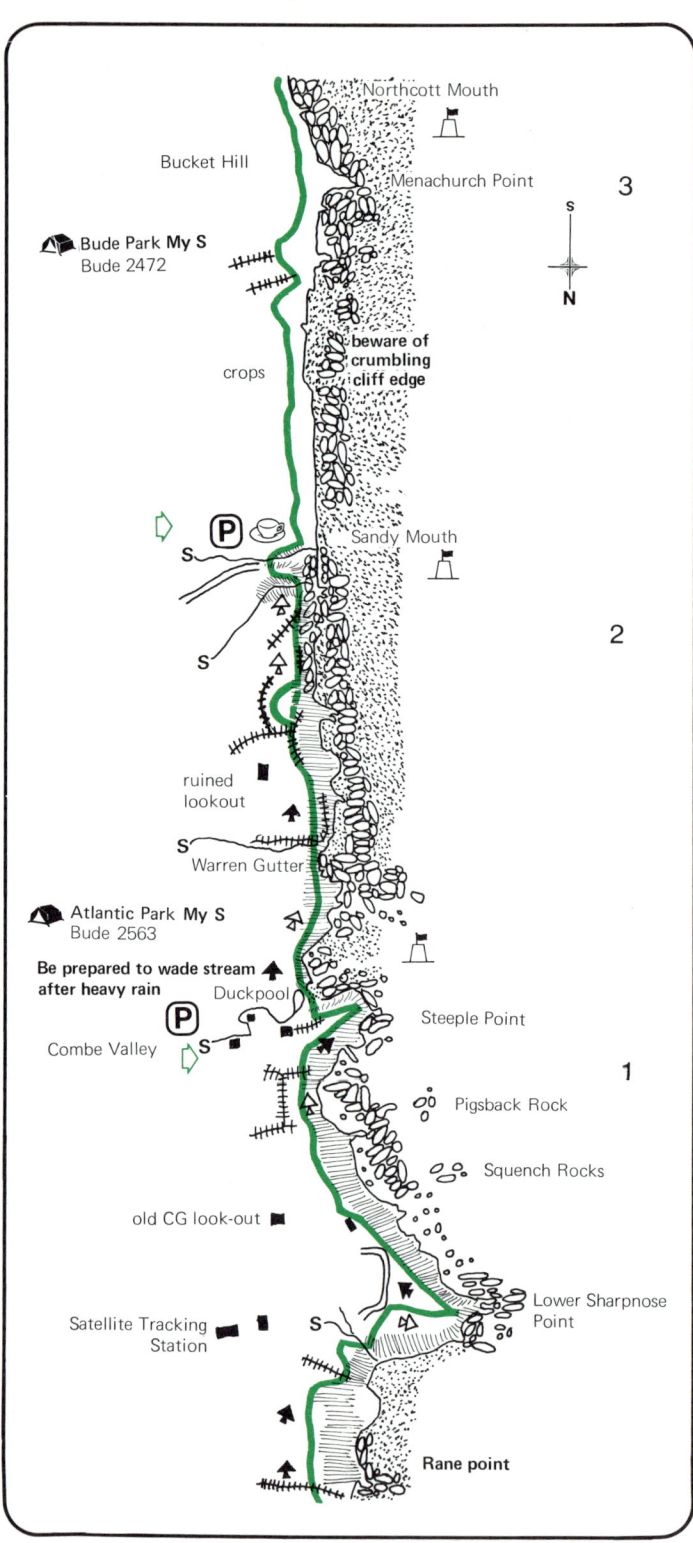

Northcott Mouth

Bucket Hill

Menachurch Point

3

Bude Park **My S**
Bude 2472

beware of crumbling cliff edge

crops

P ☕

S

Sandy Mouth

2

S

ruined lookout

S

Warren Gutter

Atlantic Park **My S**
Bude 2563

Be prepared to wade stream after heavy rain

Duckpool

Steeple Point

P

Combe Valley S

1

Pigsback Rock

Squench Rocks

old CG look-out

Satellite Tracking Station S

Lower Sharpnose Point

Rane point

17. Stanbury Mouth-Northcott Mouth

3½ miles 5½km From Minehead 67¾ miles 109km

Going: a well walked Path with fewer steep gradients than on the previous section.

Once at thé bottom of the wide valley at Stanbury Mouth (section 16) the Path up the opposite side continues over rough heathland, past the Tracking Station where signposts direct you through the area of the former army camp and a disused Coast Guard Lookout, and on, close to the cliff, to Combe Valley. The official Path runs diagonally inland down the side of the valley but for the sure-footed there is a steep zig-zag path going out to Steeple Point before it drops down to Duckpool Beach (no facilities apart from a car park). The fine sandy beach fringed on each side by rocks is a popular one. *From the height of Steeple Point, looking inland, can be seen the verdant Combe Valley owned by the National Trust. The farm above the valley on the south side is Stowe Barton (Barton=farmstead). The stables of the farm are the only remaining parts of a grand 17th-century house built by the Grenville family after the Restoration. Nearby was Stowe, home of Sir Richard Grenville, the West Country Elizabethan hero who was in charge of the ships on Raleigh's first expedition to Virginia in 1585 and whose career and dramatic death are so vividly described in A L Rowse's* Sir Richard Grenville of the Revenge. *This work gives an absorbing account of how the men of Cornwall stood up to the challenge of Spain when the Armada threatened.* The Path continues, over Stowe Cliff, before descending to Sandy Mouth, another popular beach, with refreshment booth and a car park.

From Sandy Mouth the going is less precipitous and in ½ hour you are at Northcott Mouth (teas, etc) where at low tide there is a beautiful stretch of wide sand. If you are walking on the sands make sure of the state of the tide as they are covered at high water. You can walk all the way to Bude (1 mile) if the tide conditions are right. See p 8 for hints on how to find out times of high and low tide.

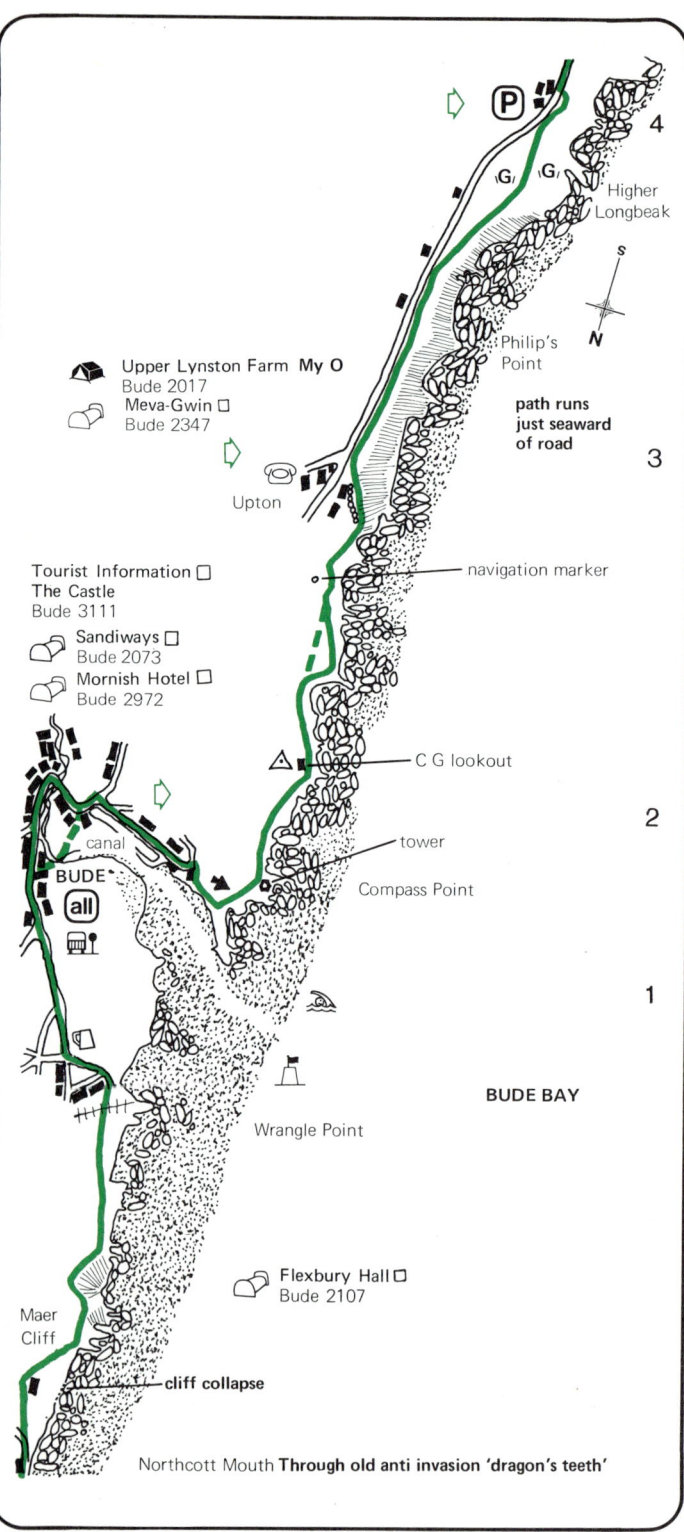

Upper Lynston Farm **My O**
Bude 2017
Meva-Gwin □
Bude 2347

Upton

Tourist Information □
The Castle
Bude 3111

Sandiways □
Bude 2073
Mornish Hotel □
Bude 2972

canal

BUDE

all

navigation marker

C G lookout

tower

Compass Point

BUDE BAY

Wrangle Point

Flexbury Hall □
Bude 2107

Maer
Cliff

cliff collapse

Higher
Longbeak

Philip's
Point

**path runs
just seaward
of road**

Northcott Mouth **Through old anti invasion 'dragon's teeth'**

4

3

2

1

18. Northcott Mouth-Bude-Higher Longbeak
4 miles 6½km   From Minehead 71¾ miles 115½km

Going: at first, a mile of cliff walking before coming to Bude
and then an uninspiring stretch spoilt by the proximity of the
road, with houses a few feet from the cliff edge.

*Bude (pop 5700), a small town with little trace of its past, is
now a popular resort. It is joined to Stratton with its Norman
church and old pub, The Tree. The Tree was the Royalist HQ
during the Battle of Stamford Hill (above Stratton) in 1643
when the Cavaliers, under Sir Bevil Grenville—descendent of
the famous Sir Richard—who was killed later at the Battle
of Lansdown, defeated the Parliamentary forces. A hero of
the occasion was Anthony Payne, a Cornish giant, who
lived at The Tree. The Bude Canal was built in 1825 to
transport sand to Launceston but now only 2 miles are
navigable. Instead of locks it raised the water by inclined
planes. The 'Castle', now council offices, was built in 1830 by
Sir Goldsworthy Gurney, the Cornish inventor and friend of
Trevithick. Responsible for a vast range of inventions, he is
said to have pioneered, with the Castle, a method of building
on sand with concrete foundations. Bude is a popular surfing
centre.*

*A feature of the beach from Bude southwards are the
outcrops of all sizes and shapes of rocks etched by the
selective action of sea and weather working along the softer
shale outcrops, leaving the more resistant sandstone and
locally limestone bands upstanding.*

For the Coast Path at Bude, cross the bridge over the river
and make for 'The Castle' (council offices) on your right. Cross
the canal, and by the Lifeboat Station the Path will be seen
leading up to the tower on the cliff through a kissing-gate. A
pleasant walk follows the cliff over Efford Down until the road
with its houses almost crowds the Path off the scene. You have
to bear with this for 1½ miles until you come to Widemouth
Sand.

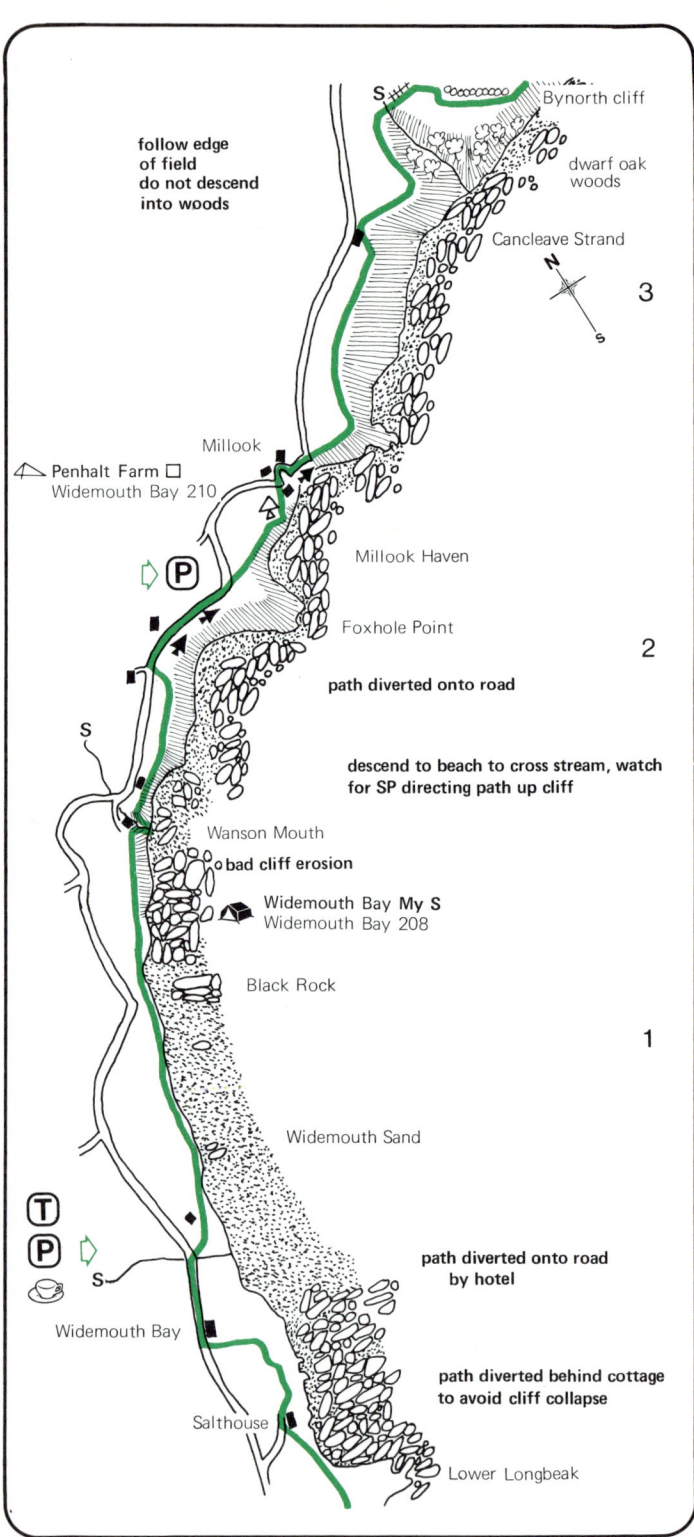

follow edge
of field
do not descend
into woods

S

Bynorth cliff

dwarf oak
woods

Cancleave Strand

N

S

3

Millook

Penhalt Farm □
Widemouth Bay 210

P

Millook Haven

Foxhole Point

2

path diverted onto road

**descend to beach to cross stream, watch
for SP directing path up cliff**

S

Wanson Mouth

bad cliff erosion

Widemouth Bay **My S**
Widemouth Bay 208

Black Rock

1

Widemouth Sand

T

P

S

**path diverted onto road
by hotel**

Widemouth Bay

**path diverted behind cottage
to avoid cliff collapse**

Salthouse

Lower Longbeak

19. Widemouth Sand-Bynorth Cliff

3½ miles 5½km   From Minehead 75¼ miles 121km

Going: the Coast Path struggles to assert itself where the road allows until Widemouth Sand. After Widemouth you will find some fine cliff scenery and some steepish gradients. There are no facilities for refreshment between Widemouth and Crackington Haven (next section) and then only during pub opening hours.

The Path takes you along the low cliff above the broad sands of Widemouth Bay past the old 'Salthouse' cottage, or you can walk along the sands. At Wanson Mouth a cliff fall makes for careful negotiation. The Path begins to climb here and soon the caravans and bungalows of Widemouth are out of sight. The scene becomes wilder with fine views of cliff and sea, descending eventually to the small bay at Millook Haven (private beach).

The cliff which you have just come down is much photographed for the extraordinary zig-zag formations of the rock strata, sandstones, and shales, which can be seen from the road at the Haven.

Follow the road which climbs steeply out of Millook Haven. At the top of the rise you will see the Path on the right of the road. From here the route lies along the cliff-top pastures.

When you come to a wooded combe cut by a small stream, note that the Path turns inland along the edge of the meadow before crossing the stream. Do not attempt to go down the cliff through the wood.

This wood of stunted sessile oaks is of interest as it is the only one in Cornwall to survive the coastal gales and the extensive felling for bark for use in tanning.

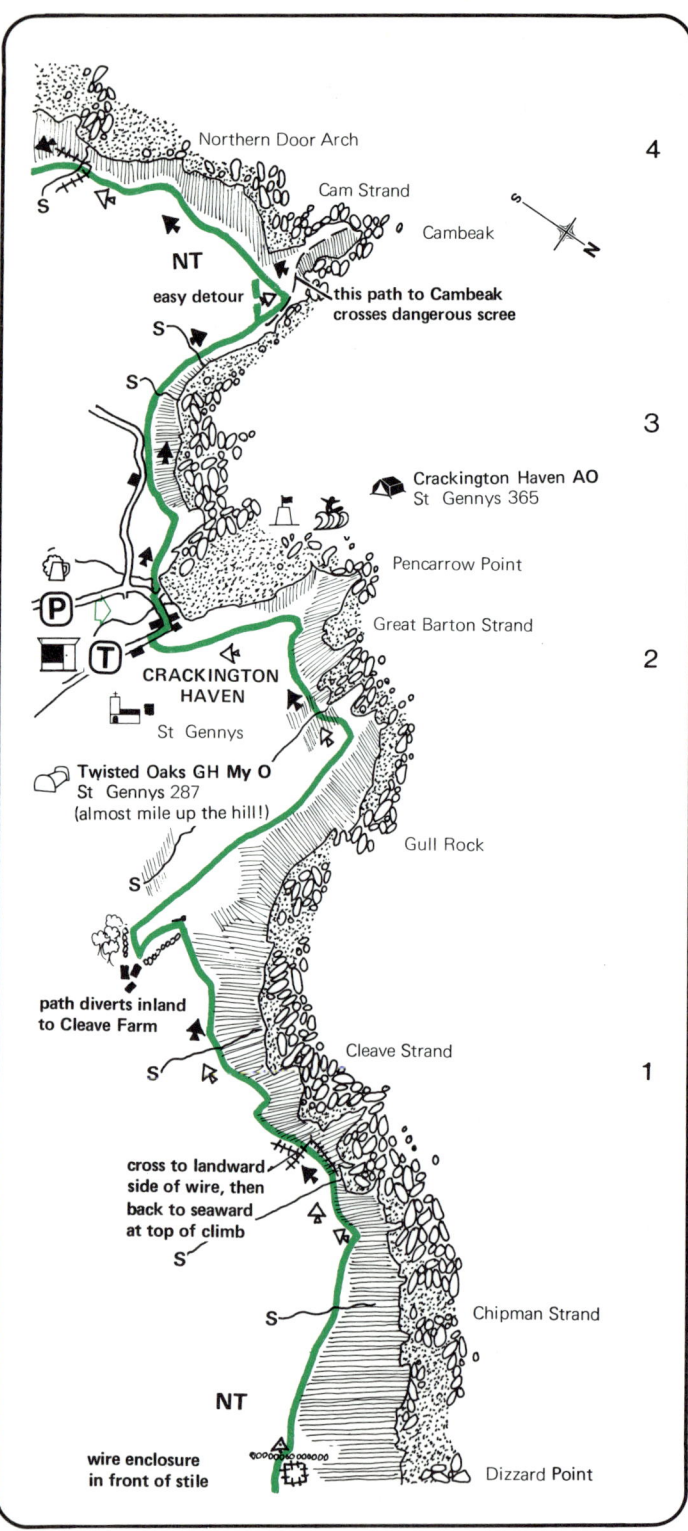

Northern Door Arch

Cam Strand

Cambeak

NT

easy detour

this path to Cambeak crosses dangerous scree

Crackington Haven **AO**
St Gennys 365

Pencarrow Point

Great Barton Strand

CRACKINGTON HAVEN

St Gennys

Twisted Oaks GH **My O**
St Gennys 287
(almost mile up the hill!)

Gull Rock

path diverts inland to Cleave Farm

Cleave Strand

cross to landward side of wire, then back to seaward at top of climb

Chipman Strand

NT

wire enclosure in front of stile

Dizzard Point

20. Dizzard Point-Crackington Haven-Northern Door Arch

4¼ miles 7km From Minehead 79½ miles 128km

Going: a wild part of the coastline—fine walking with some steep gradients. There are no places for refreshment after Crackington Haven on the 10 miles before you get to Boscastle (next section).

You walk along the edge of rough pastureland for some time without sighting any human habitation. About 1 mile from Dizzard Point the Path turns inland for a short way towards Cleave Farm to join a track taking you seawards above a steep combe. Where the track finishes on the dizzy edge of the cliff you have to drop down the sharp gradient to the bottom of the combe, fording the small stream. A climb from the stream, towards the sea, will bring you above Pencarrow Point. After rounding the 400ft headland a track runs diagonally straight down the hillside into Crackington Haven. *The huge 430ft cliffs, with their strangely contorted rock strata, tower above the small collection of houses, pub—the Combe Barton—and village stores which compose Crackington Haven. The church of St Gennys, of 11th-century foundation, lies in an idyllic situation at the end of a lane 1 mile away, and is worth a visit, if you have time. Surfing on Crackington Beach.*

From the beach the route of the Path is clear, running over the gorse-covered cliff fringing the south shore, climbing gradually until the sharp headland, Cambeak is rounded. Below, a little farther on, is a small rock arch known as Northern Door, and then the menacing line of rock, Samphire Rock, juts out on the Beach.

West from above Crackington Haven, 3 miles of coast, apart from a small gap, is owned by the National Trust, most of it a magnificent gift in memory of an aircrew lost during the Second World War.

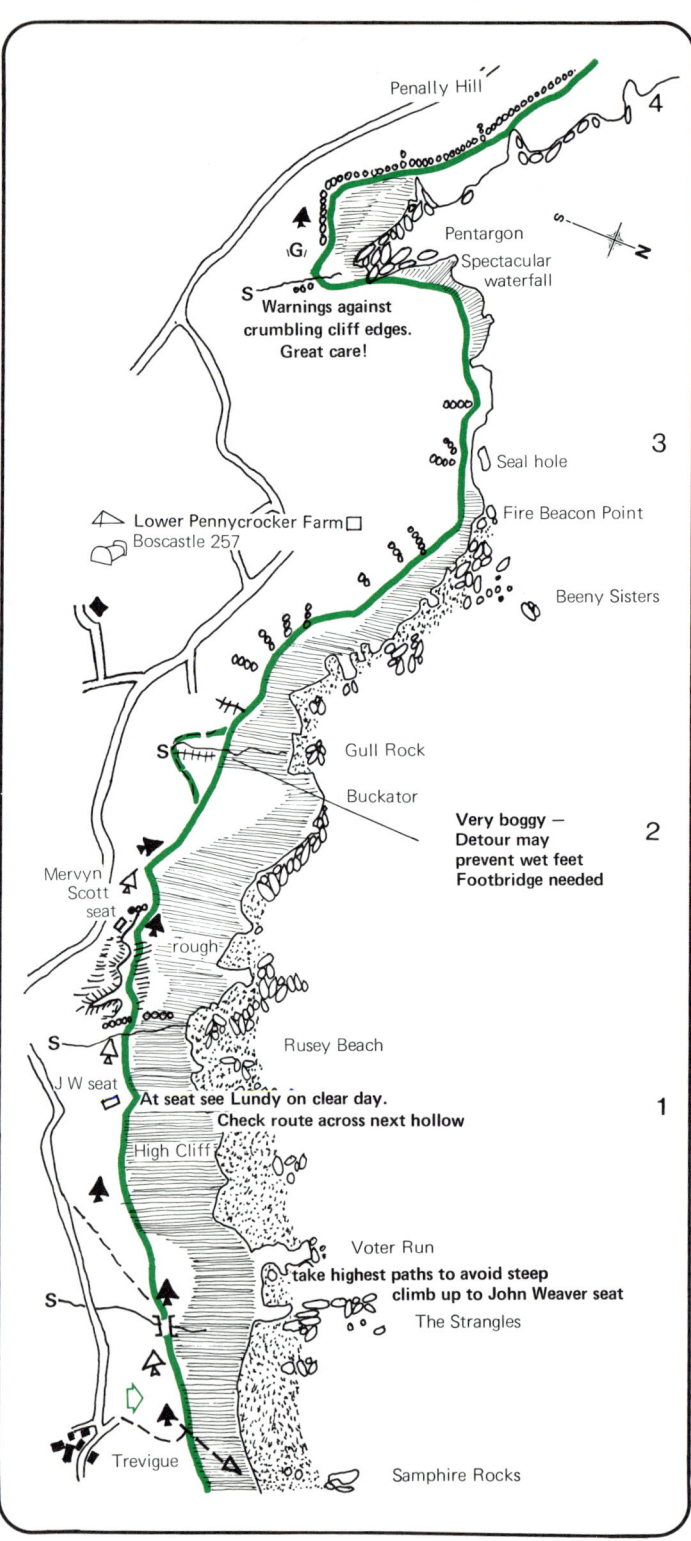

Penally Hill

4

Pentargon

Spectacular
waterfall

S

**Warnings against
crumbling cliff edges.
Great care!**

3

Seal hole

Fire Beacon Point

Lower Pennycrocker Farm
Boscastle 257

Beeny Sisters

S

Gull Rock

Buckator

**Very boggy —
Detour may
prevent wet feet
Footbridge needed**

2

Mervyn
Scott
seat

rough

S

Rusey Beach

J W seat

1

**At seat see Lundy on clear day.
Check route across next hollow**

High Cliff

Voter Run

S

**take highest paths to avoid steep
climb up to John Weaver seat**

The Strangles

Trevigue

Samphire Rocks

21. Samphire Rock-Penally Hill (Boscastle)

4¼ miles 7km   From Minehead 83¾ miles 135km

Going: good cliff-top walking with steep gradients on High Cliff. Path not too clear on approach to Penally Hill.

From the cliff-top above the Samphire Rock you have a good view of the boulder-strewn beach known as the Strangles, with a wild region of scrub between the cliff edge and the sea. At the height of a winter gale one can easily imagine the area is as lethal as it sounds and so it proved to many ships in the days of sail.

It is believed that Thomas Hardy based a scene in his early novel, A Pair of Blue Eyes, *in the Strangles. It was probably familiar to him when, as a young man working for a Dorchester architect, he was engaged in 1871–2 on restoring the church of St Juliot, near Boscastle. It was at St Juliot that he fell for the rector's sister-in-law, Emma Gifford, who became his first wife. There are paths down to the beach from the cliff.*

The Path then begins the ascent of High Cliff (731ft), the highest on the south coast if you except the Isle of Wight. The route is not as clear as could be wished: from the choice of paths keep to the highest on the hillside. There is a sharp drop the other side through the rough ground of Rusey Cliff, the south boundary of the National Trust land we have been traversing.

Across a field and the Path continues along the edge of pastureland for about 1½ miles before the slope down to Pentargon where the small stream empties onto the beach in a 120ft waterfall. After the climb out of the little valley the route follows a wall on the seaward side. You then come round Penally Hill with its prominent flagpole.

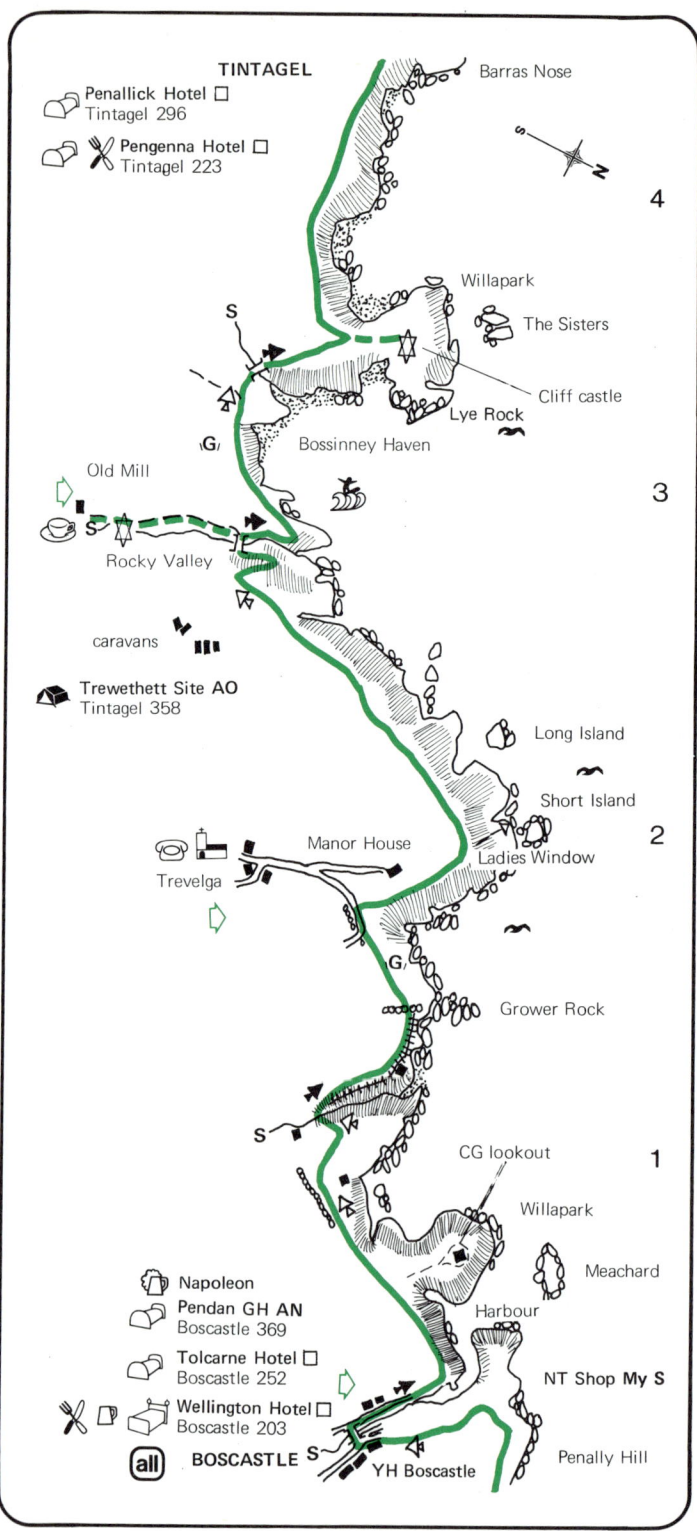

TINTAGEL

Penallick Hotel ☐
Tintagel 296

Pengenna Hotel ☐
Tintagel 223

Barras Nose

4

Willapark

The Sisters

Cliff castle

Lye Rock

Bossinney Haven

3

Old Mill

Rocky Valley

caravans

Trewethett Site **AO**
Tintagel 358

Long Island

Short Island

Manor House

Trevelga

Ladies Window

2

G

Grower Rock

CG lookout

1

Willapark

S

Meachard

Harbour

Napoleon

Pendan GH **AN**
Boscastle 369

Tolcarne Hotel ☐
Boscastle 252

Wellington Hotel ☐
Boscastle 203

all

BOSCASTLE S

YH Boscastle

NT Shop **My S**

Penally Hill

22. Penally Hill-Boscastle-Tintagel
4½ miles 7¼km From Minehead 88¼ miles 142¼km

Going: after Boscastle, a charming spot, good walking to Tintagel. At Tintagel you are likely to meet many touring sightseers in the season.

Boscastle possesses the only harbour on this coast north of Padstow. Its narrow entrance with, on each side, high cliffs of slate with lines of quartz needs careful navigation in any conditions. In the entrance is a blow-hole through which the water spouts spectacularly whenever there is a swell. The name is derived from the Bottreaux family who held the manor ('castle'—of which the only trace is a mound) in the Middle Ages. The harbour was built by the famous Sir Richard Grenville (see section 17) in Elizabeth I's reign. The steep village street is lined on each side with old lime-washed and thatched houses, a photographer's delight. Pubs: the 16th-century Napoleon at the top of the hill, used for recruiting in the Napoleonic Wars and, down by the harbour, the Wellington, and the Cobweb. Much of the Boscastle area is owned by the National Trust which has an information office and shop on the quay where there is also the youth hostel. By a footpath up the wooded Valency valley you can reach the beautifully situated old Minster church and parts of the former monastery.

The Coast Path rises from the south side of the harbour, rounds Willapark (meaning 'lookout') and continues along the cliff, past Forrabury Common which, apparently having avoided enclosure, is still cultivated in the Celtic strip system. The prominent arched rock, the Ladies Window, is to be seen seaward of the Path. You next come to a cleft in the rocks with a stream and footbridge. This is Rocky Valley and a diversion along the wooded footpath following the stream is rewarding. *In a ruined mill some way up the path there are on the rock two circular 'maze' type carvings about 9in across which may be Bronze Age. Where the stream runs under the road there is Trevilett Mill which has been restored and contains much of the workings of the old Mill. Refreshments are obtainable. Continuing up the footpath on the other side of the road, through the woods, you come, after about 1 mile, to the impressive waterfall St Nectan's Kieve and the site of a 6th-century shrine. Allow 1 hour to St Nectan's Kieve and back. Look out for dippers in the stream.*

The Path crosses the neck of the Willapark headland on which there was an Iron Age cliff-castle. Ahead will be seen the obtrusive bulk of the Tintagel Hotel which you can make for as the route circles it, bringing you out above the awe-inspiring site of Tintagel Castle.
Bosinney Haven has a pebble beach, popular with surfers. The village of Bosinney has a long history, Sir Walter Raleigh being its MP. Short Island, Long Island, and Lye Rock are breeding sites for sea birds. See appendix.

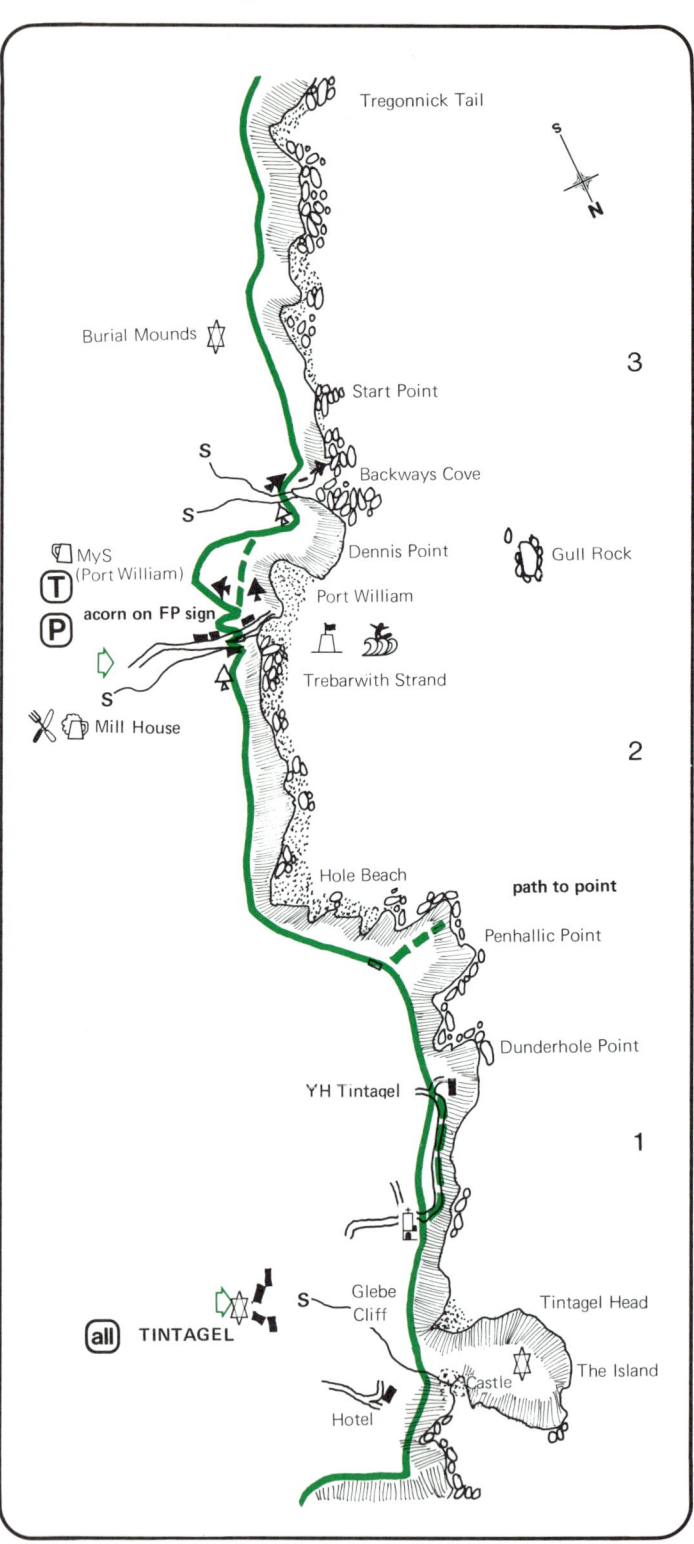

Tregonnick Tail

3

Burial Mounds

Start Point

S

S

Backways Cove

MyS
(Port William)

T

P

acorn on FP sign

Dennis Point

Gull Rock

Port William

S

Trebarwith Strand

Mill House

2

Hole Beach

path to point

Penhallic Point

Dunderhole Point

YH Tintagel

1

Glebe
Cliff

S

Tintagel Head

all TINTAGEL

The Island

Hotel

Castle

23. Tintagel-Trebarwith Strand-Tregonnick Tail

3¾ miles 6km   From Minehead 92 miles 148¼km

Going: a wild part of the coast with one steep climb at Backways Cove. The route of Path not very clear in one place; follow instructions given below. Fine views.

Present-day Tintagel is founded on the King Arthur myth. Historical evidence about Arthur is extremely sparse but it seems he was a hero when Britain was struggling in the Dark Ages after the Romans left. Arthur's link with Tintagel was first mentioned in the 12th century by Geoffrey of Monmouth and, in view of what is perhaps the most dramatic setting in Britain, Tennyson and others have copied it. Apart from the Old Post Office—actually a small 15th-century Cornish manor house—there is nothing distinguished about the village which is full of tourist attractions such as the Excalibar pub. However the Island itself is most impressive. Even more emotive than the Castle ruins are the traces of a Celtic monastery which was quite likely founded in c AD 500 by the Welsh missionary St Juliot. The first castle, of which parts of the Great Hall still stand, was built in the 12th century by the illegitimate son of Henry I, Reginald de Cornwall, and additions were made by the Black Prince in the 14th century. The Castle was later used as a prison and by the 16th century had become a ruin. A booklet is available from the Department of the Environment.

The Coast Path climbs up south of the Castle Site.
Tintagel church of St Materiana, Norman with parts believed to be earlier, can be visited by a short detour.

At Dunderhole Point you come to the Tintagel Youth Hostel whose site, with its sea views, must be the grandest of all British Youth Hostels. It is housed in former slate quarry offices.

The Path continues close to the edge of the cliffs where until 50 years ago slate was blasted. At Hole Beach is a curious high pillar of rock said to have been left purposely by the quarrymen as a shelter. Trebarwith Strand (Port William) formerly shipped slate—the slipway is on the south side where there are impressive caves. Sands are uncovered at low tide. Surfing. Pub: Port William (summer).
Half a mile inland a fine old mill is the site of the Mill House pub, open all the year.

The Path is signposted leading off the drive of the Port William pub and rounds the base of the 300ft hill dominating the beach on the south. You come out above the wild, lonely Backways Cove; a track leads to the bridge over the stream. The Path runs up the steep south side of the valley but if you make for the prominent rock halfway up the slope a clearer track leads diagonally seawards to the crest. On top there are two Bronze Age burial mounds. The Path from here is unclear but walk through the gorse, parallel to the cliff. You come to a fence; the Path continues round the seaward end of it.

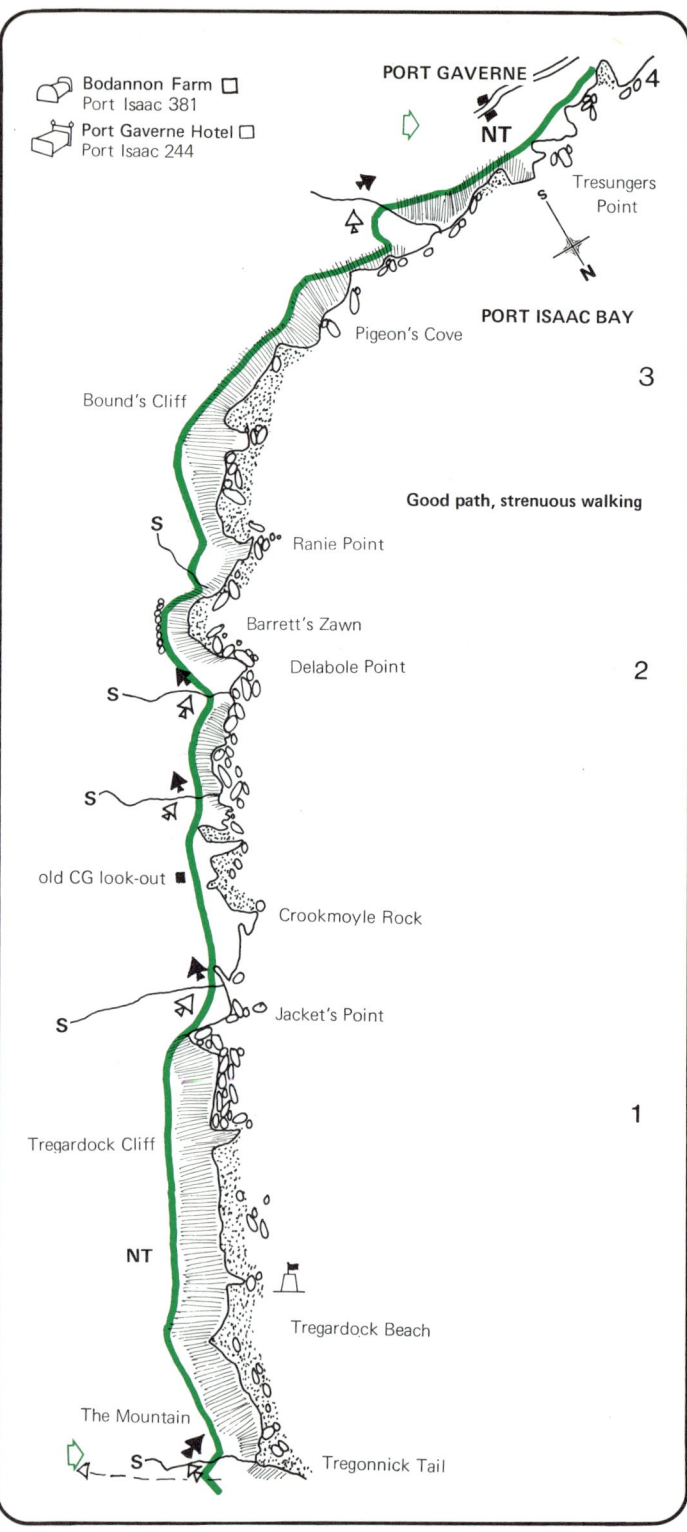

Bodannon Farm □
Port Isaac 381

Port Gaverne Hotel □
Port Isaac 244

PORT GAVERNE

NT

Tresungers
Point

PORT ISAAC BAY

Pigeon's Cove

Bound's Cliff

Good path, strenuous walking

S

Ranie Point

Barrett's Zawn

Delabole Point

S

S

old CG look-out ■

Crookmoyle Rock

S

Jacket's Point

Tregardock Cliff

NT

Tregardock Beach

The Mountain

S

Tregonnick Tail

4

3

2

1

24. Tregardock Beach-Port Gaverne
4 miles 6½km From Minehead 96 miles 154¾km

Going: a wild and unspoiled stretch with some steep combes to negotiate. Path clear and going good.

The Path, from the fence mentioned in the last section, proceeds in the narrow space available along the cliff edge and brings you out to the headland, Tregonnick Tail, above Tregardock Beach which is a tumbled break in the cliffs, dominated by a large 'hump'—the 'Mountain'—round which the Path winds.

Tregardock Cliff is National Trust land with access from a farm off the B 3314 road. There is a sandy beach for a few hours at low water. Swimming and surfing should be reserved for the experts.

Once past Tregardock the Path drops steeply down to the bottom of a little combe—you cross the stream by edging along the fence—continues up the other side, close to the cliff edge for some distance, past a disused Coast Guard lookout (keep seaward of the fence), and down to a wide valley.

On the south side of the valley is what seems to be a cave entrance. It is actually the entrance to a tunnel (now unusable) leading down to the next beach, Barrett's Zawn (zawn = chasm), through which slate was drawn from a beach quarry.

Round the spectacular Barrett's Zawn and the Path goes down another steep little valley whose banks in spring are covered in primroses, along Bounds Cliff, and drops down to Port Gaverne and the Port Gaverne Hotel, a charming place.

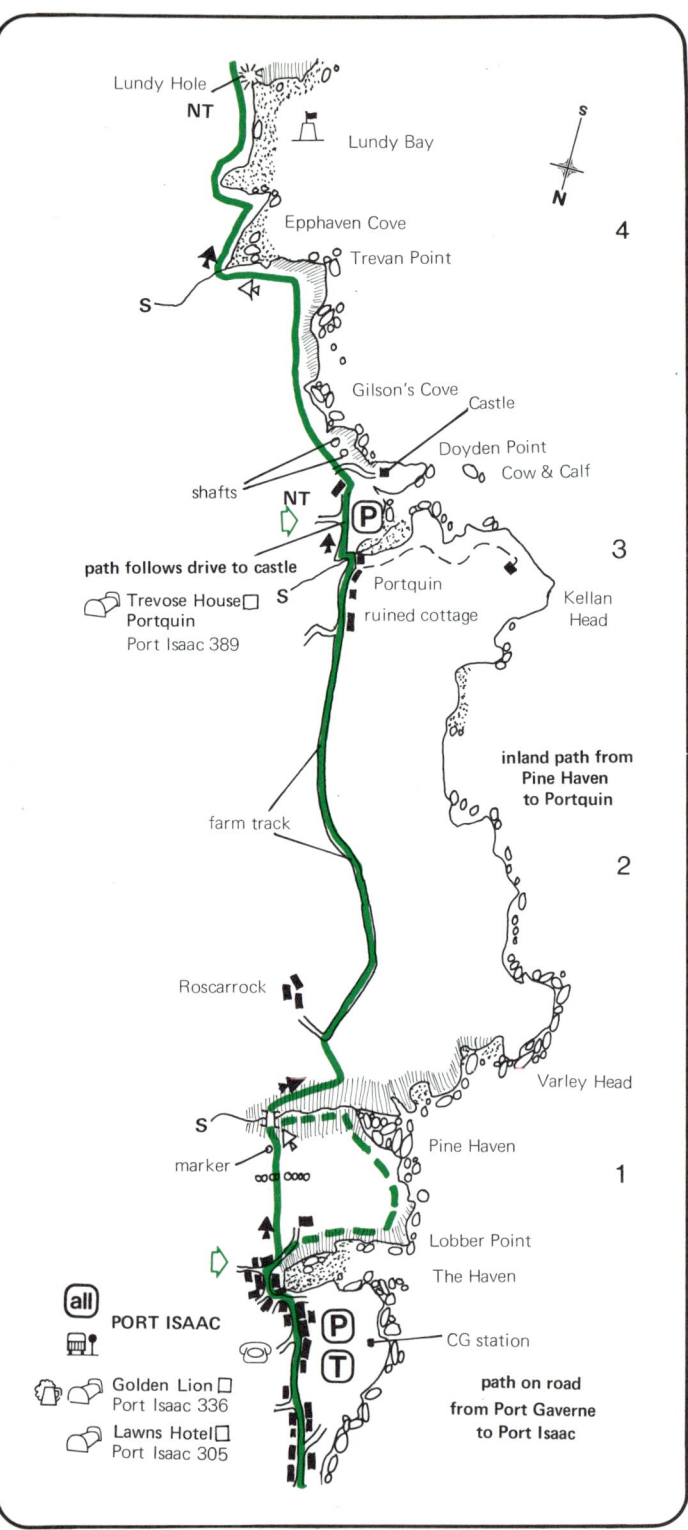

Lundy Hole

NT

Lundy Bay

Epphaven Cove

Trevan Point

S

Gilson's Cove

Castle

Doyden Point

Cow & Calf

shafts

NT

P

path follows drive to castle

S

Portquin

Trevose House
Portquin
Port Isaac 389

ruined cottage

Kellan
Head

**inland path from
Pine Haven
to Portquin**

farm track

Roscarrock

Varley Head

S

Pine Haven

marker

Lobber Point

The Haven

all

PORT ISAAC

P
T

CG station

Golden Lion
Port Isaac 336

Lawns Hotel
Port Isaac 305

**path on road
from Port Gaverne
to Port Isaac**

N   S

4

3

2

1

25. Port Gaverne-Port Isaac-Lundy Bay
4¾ miles 7¾km From Minehead 100¾ miles 162¼km

Going: the Path follows the road for ½ mile to Port Isaac and then due to an obstruction on the coast, is diverted inland to Portquin. From there a pleasant cliff path to Lundy Bay.

Port Isaac is only a few minutes up the road from Port Gaverne.

Port Isaac (from the Cornish for 'corn port') is one of the most picturesque of Cornish fishing villages. Its small quay, built in the 15th century, is no longer so busy with fishing boats but round the harbour the old houses look much the same as in the old days. The narrow streets and passages, one only 1½ft wide, 'Squeezibelly Ally', always delight the visitor.

Follow the 'public footpath' sign which stands at the foot of the narrow street which climbs out of the little town on the south side of the Harbour. From there the Path is well signposted all the way to Portquin, rounding Lobber Point before crossing the stream by a footbridge. It then turns inland passing close to the farm of Rosscarrock, parts of which are said to be 12th century, and continues across the fields, eventually coming out on the road just above Portquin. The field path tends to get very muddy in wet weather.

A few yards down the road on the right is the ivy-covered ruin of a small house. Inside you can see how it has been built of local slate, using also the rock for a wall. Portquin has a few cottages and a long derelict building once used for salting fish. There are various accounts of why the village became deserted, one being that all the men were drowned when trying to elude an 18th-century press gang but the answer is probably that, as elsewhere, the shoals disappeared. There are no facilities for food in the village.

Take the road out of Portquin; near the top of the rise the Path leads off to seaward, past a National Trust house.

On Doyden Point is a 19th-century 'folly', Doyden Castle, in which the owner used to stage parties.

By the next stile on the Path is the old shaft of an antimony mine, fenced round.

The Path, good with fine views, continues along the cliffs, all in National Trust territory, bringing you to Lundy Bay, an excellent sandy beach in quiet and green surroundings.

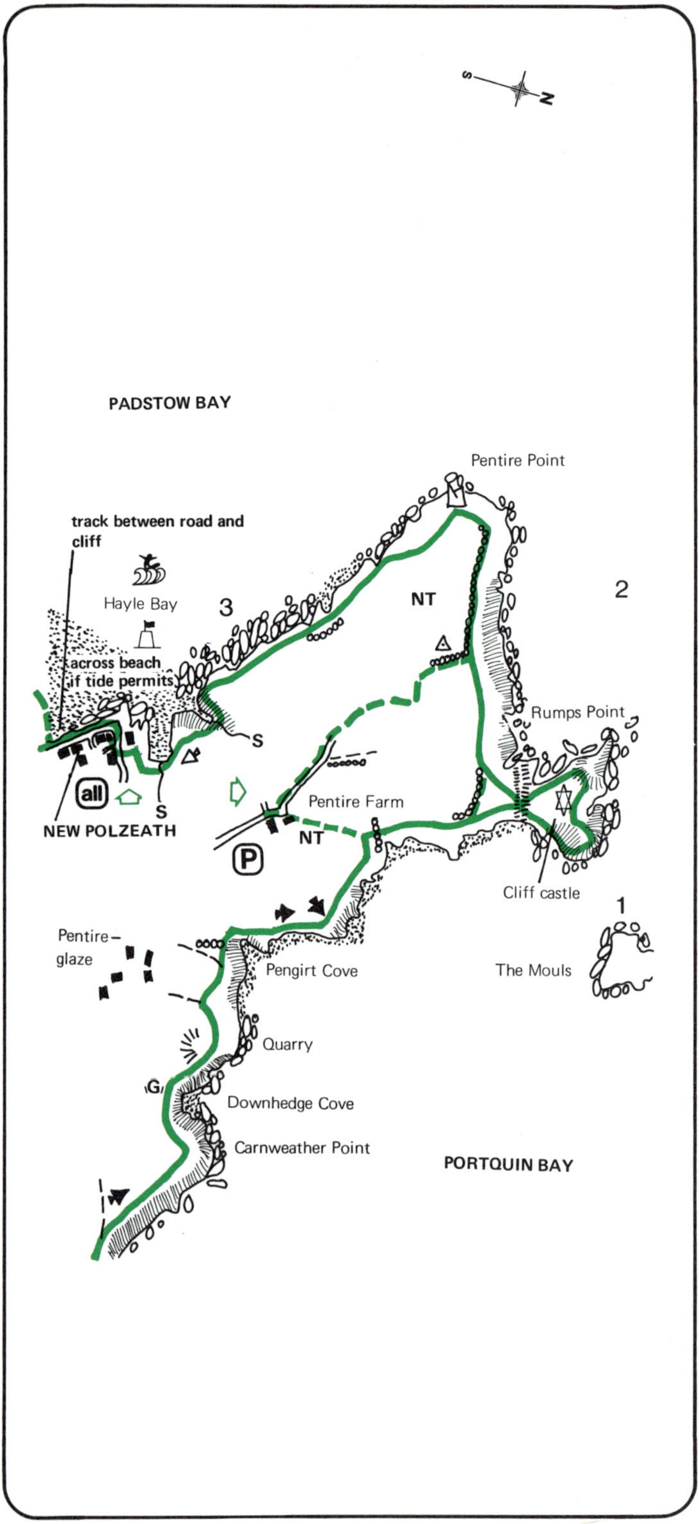

PADSTOW BAY

Pentire Point

track between road and
cliff

Hayle Bay

3

NT

2

across beach
if tide permits

S

Rumps Point

S

Pentire Farm

P

NT

Cliff castle

1

Pentire-
glaze

Pengirt Cove

The Mouls

Quarry

G

Downhedge Cove

Carnweather Point

PORTQUIN BAY

NEW POLZEATH

all

S

60

26. Portquin Bay-New Polzeath

3¾ miles 6km From Minehead 104½ miles 168¼ km

Going: fine varied walking with no problems.

From Lundy Bay the National Trust has well signposted the Path; where the route branches the sign directs you round Carnweather Point towards Rumps Point, climbing through the gorse above Portquin Bay.

The landscape, coastal and inland, has changed. The cliffs are not so high, and the countryside gentler and softer than on the previous 50 miles.

The cliff Path turns east above the headland of Rumps Point. *The outline of the impressive Rumps Point cliff castle, a fortified settlement of the Iron Age or even earlier, can be seen to advantage from the Path: a triple rampart across the neck of the headland defended access; the position of the entrances can also be made out. Excavations have produced pottery of the 1st century BC to the 1st century AD.*

On, round Pentire Head, follow the Path high through sheep pasture. *The rock formation has changed. The sedimentary slates and shales have given place to igneous rocks, ie rocks that were once molten. The rocks at Pentire Point itself are magnificent pillow lavas representing the fossilized outpourings of a once massive submarine volcano.*

You now turn south-east and drop down to Pentireglaze Haven where there is a small sandy beach. The Path then climbs steeply for the short distance to the road above and the terrace of houses facing Hayle Bay in New Polzeath (the Atlantic Hotel, the only pub in the resort, occupies one of these houses).

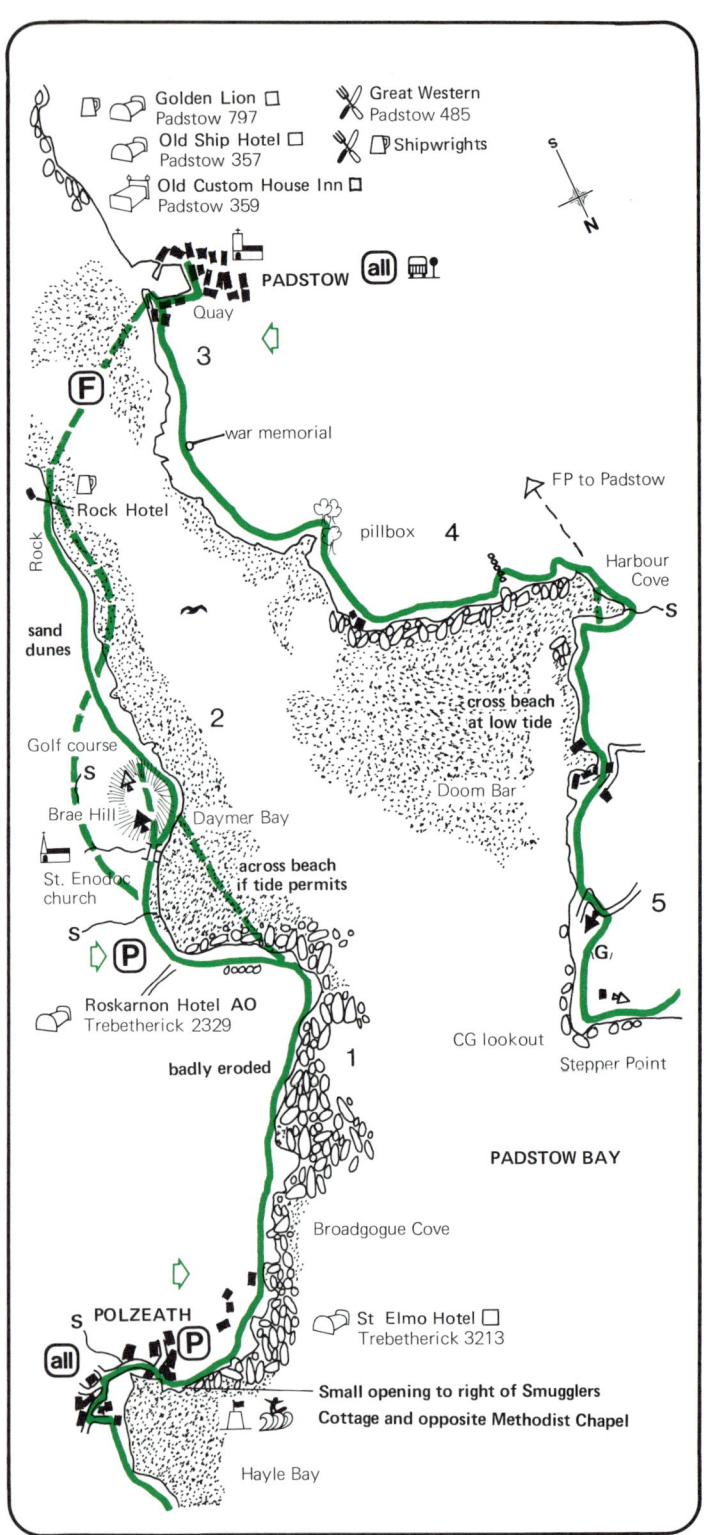

Golden Lion
Padstow 797

Old Ship Hotel
Padstow 357

Old Custom House Inn
Padstow 359

Great Western
Padstow 485

Shipwrights

PADSTOW [all]

Quay

3

war memorial

F

Rock Hotel

Rock

sand
dunes

2

Golf course

S

Brae Hill

St. Enodoc
church

S

P

Roskarnon Hotel AO
Trebetherick 2329

badly eroded

Daymer Bay

across beach
if tide permits

pillbox

4

FP to Padstow

Harbour
Cove

S

cross beach
at low tide

Doom Bar

5

G

CG lookout

Stepper Point

1

PADSTOW BAY

Broadgogue Cove

POLZEATH

[all]

S

P

St Elmo Hotel
Trebetherick 3213

Small opening to right of Smugglers
Cottage and opposite Methodist Chapel

Hayle Bay

27. New Polzeath-Padstow-Stepper Point

5½ miles* 8¾km From Minehead 110 miles 177km

Going: quite a contrast: quiet walking along the shores of the Camel estuary, the first part adjacent to a built-up area but pleasant nevertheless.

From the terrace in New Polzeath the Path leads down through the sandhills to the resort of Polzeath at the bay's head. *Polzeath has some fine sands. Surfing.*

Take the road running south from Polzeath. A few yards up the hill, on the right, a sign directs between houses on to the Path, along a fine turf promenade known as the Greenaway, fringing the low cliff. After about 1½ miles you come to Daymer Bay with its sandy beach. The Path, after crossing a small stream is not very easy to follow but if you follow the telephone poles you will see a sign showing the way round the prominent Brae Hill. For an interesting alternative, make for the golf course ahead of you, following the path marked by white posts. *To the left of this path is the church of St Enodoc, early 15th century with a 13th-century spire, which for years was buried by encroaching sands. It is built on the site of a 6th-century oratory. Keep on the marked track which rejoins the official Path on the other side of Brae Hill.*

After crossing the boundary of a large estate the Path continues along the shore of the estuary for ¾ mile before coming to Rock where there is the passenger ferry to Padstow (frequent departures: April to October daily; November to March, weekdays only). The ferry leaves from the beach in front of Westerly Sailing School. Car park.

Padstow (pop 2800), an old fishing port with an attractive waterfront, was made a borough in 1583. The church of St Petroc, a Welsh missionary who landed near by in the 6th century, is mainly 15th century, with earlier portions; there are two very early Cornish crosses in the churchyard. Prideaux Place (1598) is still the family home. John Prideaux was on the Virginia expedition with Grenville (section 17). There are many good pubs. On Padstow's May Day Hobby Horse Festival a man dressed as a horse runs through the streets among singing crowds.

The Coast Path leads from the Harbour along North Quay, through the Deer Park (of Prideaux Place), and along the west bank of the estuary to Harbour Cove, old lifeboat station, and Stepper Point with its tower and Coast Guard lookout. *At low tide the appropriately named Doom Bar may be seen. This sandbank at the entrance of the estuary has seen the wrecking of hundreds of ships and the death of their crews, despite many heroic efforts of Padstow men to save them. A more peaceful aspect of the estuary is its wild life, particularly in winter when teal, wigeon, pintail, shoveler, scaup, goldeneye, and also many waders may be seen. Osprey are among the birds to be seen in summer.*

*not including ferry.

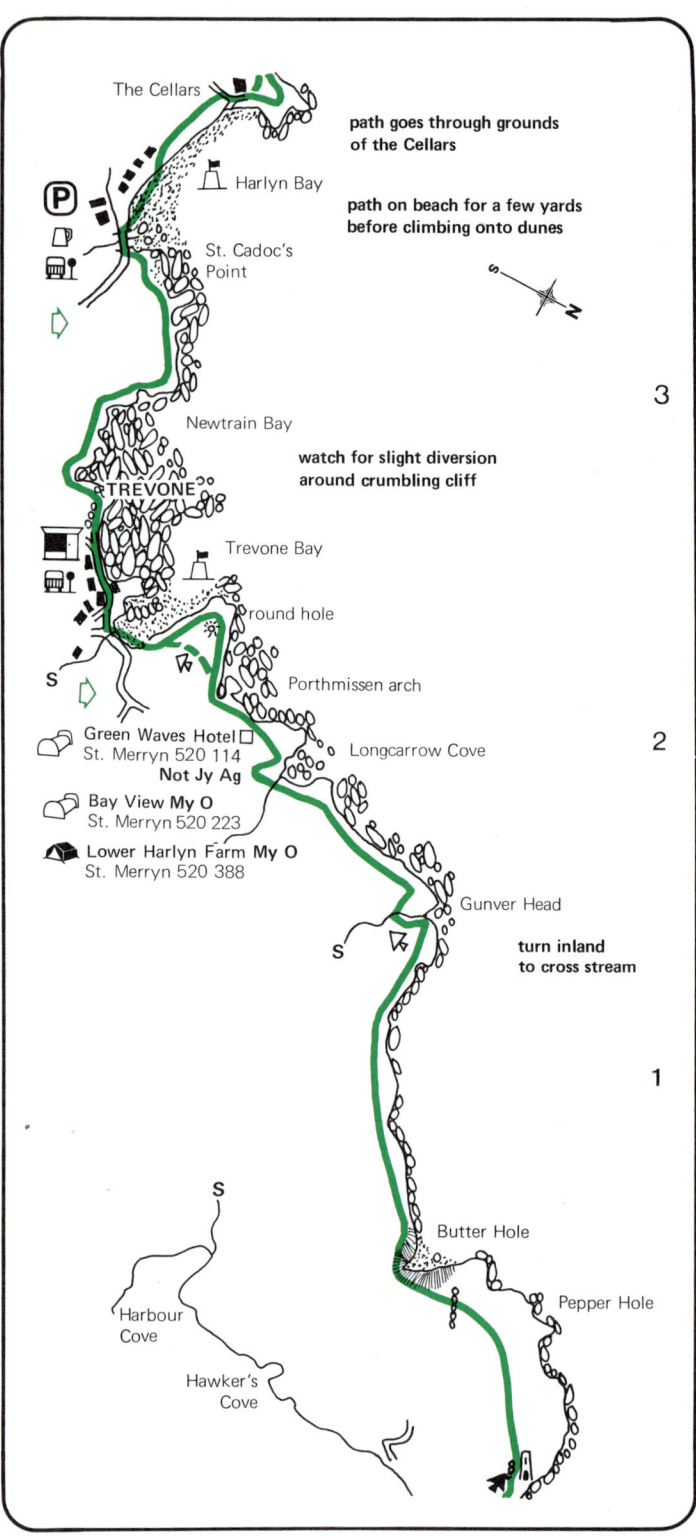

The Cellars

path goes through grounds
of the Cellars

Harlyn Bay

path on beach for a few yards
before climbing onto dunes

St. Cadoc's
Point

Newtrain Bay

watch for slight diversion
around crumbling cliff

TREVONE

Trevone Bay

round hole

Porthmissen arch

Green Waves Hotel
St. Merryn 520 114
Not Jy Ag

Longcarrow Cove

Bay View My O
St. Merryn 520 223

Lower Harlyn Farm My O
St. Merryn 520 388

Gunver Head

turn inland
to cross stream

Butter Hole

Pepper Hole

Harbour
Cove

Hawker's
Cove

3

2

1

28. Pepper Hole-Trevone-Harlyn Bay

3¾ miles 6km From Minehead 113¾ miles 183¼km

Going: good high-cliff walking to Trevone then low level to sandy Harlyn.

The Coast Path is clear from Stepper Point along the cliffs with impressive rocky views. The route passes Porthmissen, a small promontory with an arch carved by the sea and then, just seaward of the Path, 'Round Hole', where the roof of a sea cave has collapsed.

Trevone is a small popular resort with good sands. Few facilities, but two pubs at St Merryn 1¾ miles inland.

From Trevone the Path keeps to the low coastline until the sandy, sheltered Harlyn Beach is reached.

There are only a few houses at Harlyn but it is known to archaeologists for the discoveries made in the district. The most important was that in 1900 when an Iron Age cemetery with over 100 slate coffins was found containing, with human remains, a variety of bronze and iron ornaments. Until recently there was a small museum on the site but this is now closed and most of the exhibits transferred to Truro Museum. Earlier at Harlyn two beautiful Celtic gold lunulae (crescent-shaped ornaments) about 8in wide, of fine workmanship and about 3000 years old, were found. These also can be seen in Truro Museum.

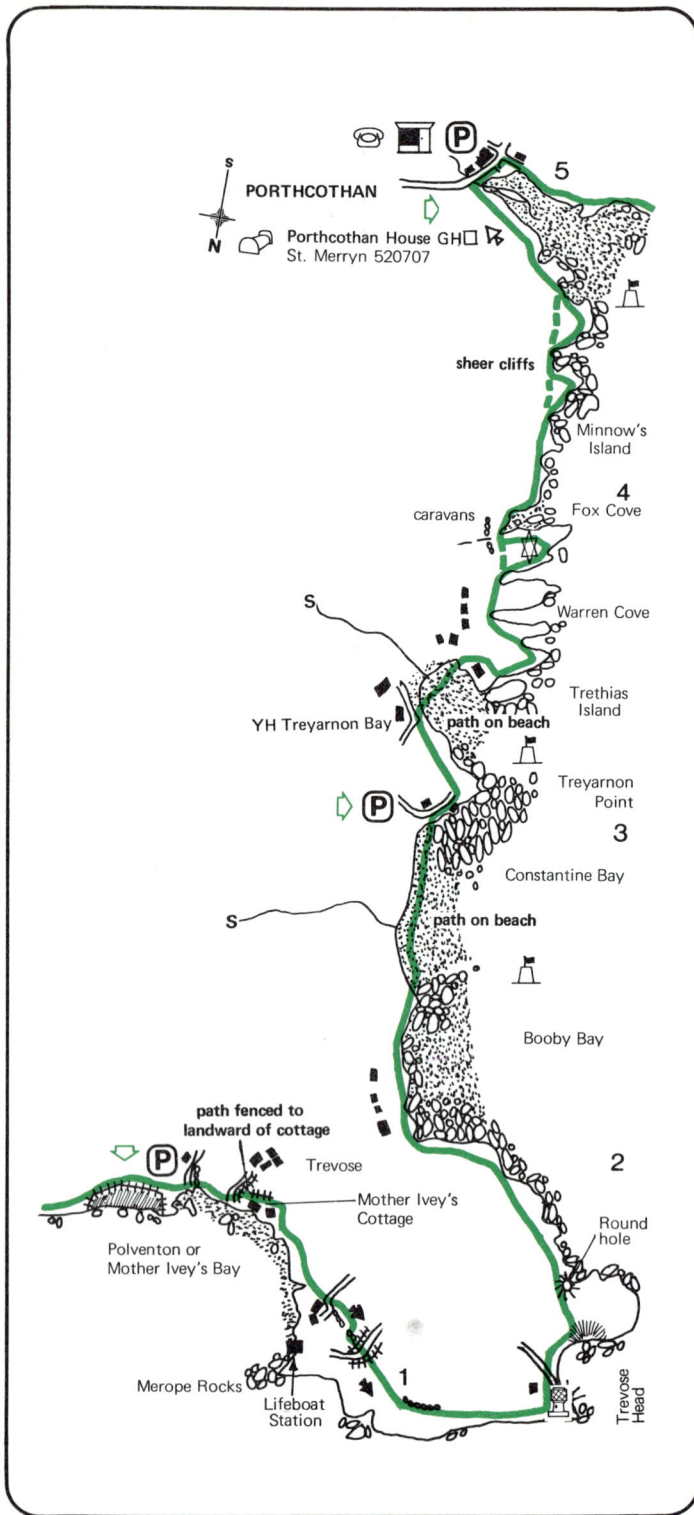

PORTHCOTHAN

Porthcothan House GH
St. Merryn 520707

5

sheer cliffs

Minnow's
Island

caravans

4 Fox Cove

Warren Cove

S

Trethias
Island

YH Treyarnon Bay

path on beach

Treyarnon
Point

P

3

Constantine Bay

S

path on beach

Booby Bay

path fenced to
landward of cottage

Trevose

P

Mother Ivey's
Cottage

Round
hole

2

Polventon or
Mother Ivey's Bay

Merope Rocks

Lifeboat
Station

1

Trevose
Head

29. Polventon Bay-Porthcothan

5½ miles 8¾km From Minehead 119¼ miles 192km

Going: a section of contrasts, with no problems. Almost at sea-level at Polventon Bay and then up to the 240ft headland of Trevose Head; round the low-lying shores of Constantine and Treyarnon Bays with an easy ascent to the cliff top above Porthcothan.

Just over the bridge in Harlyn, the Path leads up from the sands of the beach, by some bungalows and keeping close to the coastline, rounds Cataclews Point and Polventon (or Mother Ivey's) Bay. It passes a caravan site and Mother Ivey's cottage en route. At the far end of the Bay is the Padstow Lifeboat Station.

Trevose Head, like other headlands in the area, is composed of rocks of volcanic origin, more resistant than the sedimentary local formations, slates etc. The Lighthouse can be visited on weekday afternoons. Fine views are to be had on a clear day of the whole of the north Cornish coast from St Ives to Hartland Point.

On turning south from Trevose Head you drop down to Booby Bay and the adjacent wide Constantine Bay. Fine sands are exposed by the tide but bathing can be dangerous because of the rocks. The Path follows the dunes round the shore, or you can walk on the sands. Over a small rise you come to Treyarnon Bay where surfing is good. Treyarnon Youth Hostel is right on the Bay, overlooking the sea. From Treyarnon Bay there is an easy ascent to the top of the cliffs which although not so very high, drop sheer. After a fine cliff-top walk of about 1 mile you come to the fine beach at Porthcothan.

It was on these cliffs that the Cornish chough (a bird of the crow family), the County's emblem, last bred. It is now only found in Wales. There is one pub, the Treorea, at Porthcothan, and a place for teas in the season. Car park. Surfing.

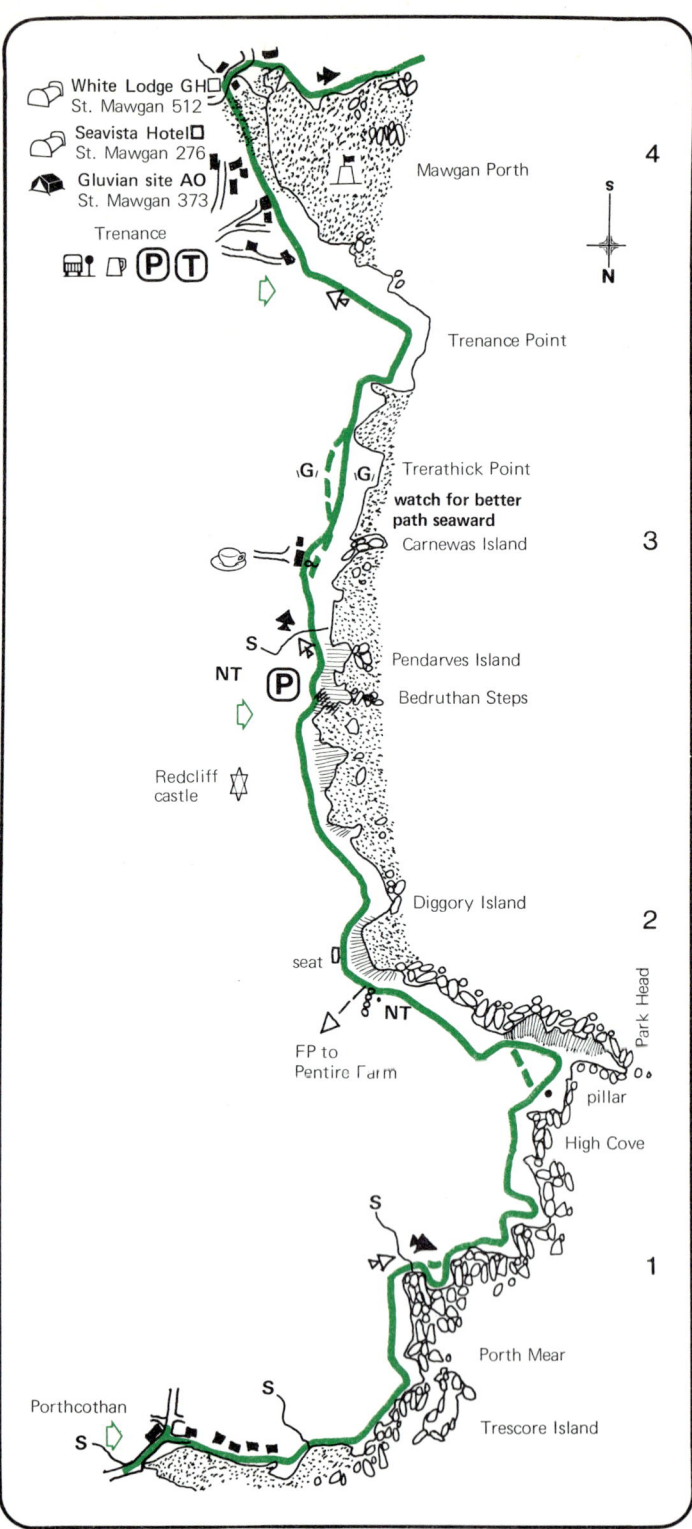

White Lodge GH
St. Mawgan 512

Seavista Hotel
St. Mawgan 276

Gluvian site AO
St. Mawgan 373

Trenance

Mawgan Porth

4

S

N

Trenance Point

Trerathick Point

watch for better
path seaward

Carnewas Island

3

Pendarves Island

NT

Bedruthan Steps

Redcliff
castle

Diggory Island

2

Park Head

seat

NT

FP to
Pentire Farm

pillar

High Cove

1

Porth Mear

Porthcothan

Trescore Island

30. Porthcothan-Bedruthan-Mawgan Porth

4½ miles 7¼km From Minehead 123¾ miles 199¼km

Going: fine straightforward cliff-top walking.

The Coast Path leads up from the road at Porthcothan along and above the south shore of the beach, past a few houses, and then climbs gradually to Park Head, National Trust land for most of the way.

After passing Park Head, a zig-zag path known as Pentire Steps leads down to the beach.

A short distance farther and you come to the famous Bedruthan Steps.

The Steps are the huge rock 'islands' of volcanic origin, left isolated on the beach through erosion. Thanks to the National Trust the steps down to the beach have now been restored after having been unusable for a long time. Care is still needed in the descent, especially by children. There are two car parks: the one on the cliff top having a refreshment booth in season. As you approach the Bedruthan area, almost on the Path itself, is Redcliffe Castle, a fine Iron Age promontory fort. The traces of the deep defensive ditch can clearly be made out. As can be well imagined, this part of the coast was a death trap to shipping in the days of sail, particularly before the Trevose lighthouse was completed in 1847. A famous incident was that of the 220-ton Samaritan, with a cargo of cotton and silks, which was wrecked off Bedruthan Steps in an October gale of 1846 with only two of the crew surviving. The local populace for months after were decked out in finery looted from the wreck which was heartlessly nicknamed the Good Samaritan. One of the Bedruthan Steps is called the Samaritan after the wreck.

Continuing from Bedruthan the Path runs through rough gorse on the cliff top down to Mawgan Porth, a bungalow resort with a good sandy beach and surfing. The Merrymore is an old fishermen's pub.

Close to the main road in the village is the site of a small 1500-year-old Dark Ages settlement and cemetery, the huts built round a courtyard. Apply to beach café or garage to view.

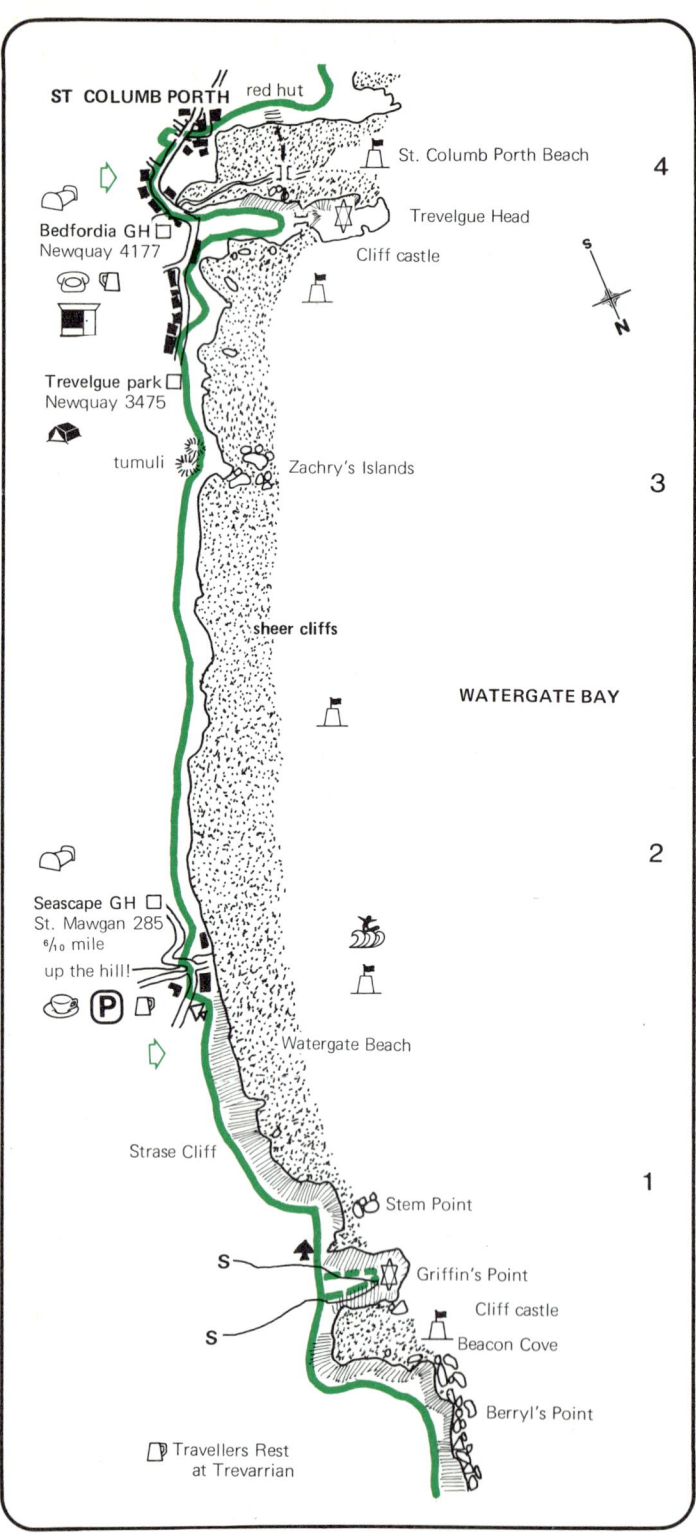

ST COLUMB PORTH   red hut

St. Columb Porth Beach

Trevelgue Head

Cliff castle

Bedfordia GH
Newquay 4177

Trevelgue park
Newquay 3475

tumuli

Zachry's Islands

sheer cliffs

WATERGATE BAY

Seascape GH
St. Mawgan 285
⁶/₁₀ mile
up the hill!

Watergate Beach

Strase Cliff

Stem Point

S

Griffin's Point

Cliff castle

S

Beacon Cove

Berryl's Point

Travellers Rest
at Trevarrian

4

3

2

1

31. Berryl's Porth-St Columb Porth (Newquay)

4½ miles 7¼km   From Minehead 128¼ miles 206½km

Going: easy walking along the 200ft cliff above the 2-mile-long Watergate Beach. You are approaching Newquay and a very popular part of the coast with crowded beaches, etc, in the summer—although there is plenty of room on Watergate.

Over the bridge at Mawgan Porth, the road climbs steeply. The Path turns off the road on the right and leads to the cliff-top at Berryl's Point. You round Beacon Cove (steep path down to the beach) and then across the neck of the headland, Griffin's Point.

On Griffin's Point is another well defined Iron Age fortification with two ramparts and ditches.

At Watergate there is a gap in the cliff and access to the wide sands of Watergate (or Tregurrian) Beach. This is a favourite for surfing enthusiasts. Hotel and car park. From here you can either walk along the cliff top or on the sands. As you approach Newquay you will come to the promontory Trevelgue Head, the landward half occupied by a putting-green.

At Trevelgue Head is the most impressive of all the Cornish 'cliff castles'. As you walk to the point of the Head you pass six ramparts and ditches, the last two on the island connected to the 'mainland' by a footbridge. Excavations have produced evidence of occupation from the Bronze Age (about 2000 BC) to Roman times.

Porth (or St Columb Porth), now a district of Newquay, has a fine sandy beach at low tide. Follow the road round the beach (or you can cross the sands), past Porth House Hotel, down steps on the left and under the road bridge. The Path then leads up along a cliff overlooking the beach, turning south to join Lusty Glaze Road, and so into Newquay.

Newquay: authority was given in 1439 by the Bishop of Exeter to the inhabitants of the small fishing hamlet of Towan Blistra to build a new quay. However, the earliest traces of human settlement are on Trevelgue Head—and in the town itself on Barrowfields, where the Coast Path enters the centre of Newquay, there are three tumuli or burial mounds, probably 2,500 years old.

After the new quay was built, local trade grew, and fishing —particularly of pilchards. On the cliff above the harbour is the well preserved Huer's House from which the 'huer', on spotting the shoals of fish, would call out to direct the fishermen.

In the last century Newquay also imported coal for the nearby tin and copper mines, and engaged in coastal trade generally. But by the end of the century its livelihood came to depend more on the holidaymakers attracted by its five wide sandy beaches which, today, offer surfing and supervised bathing. With a population of 15,000 it is now north Cornwall's most important resort.

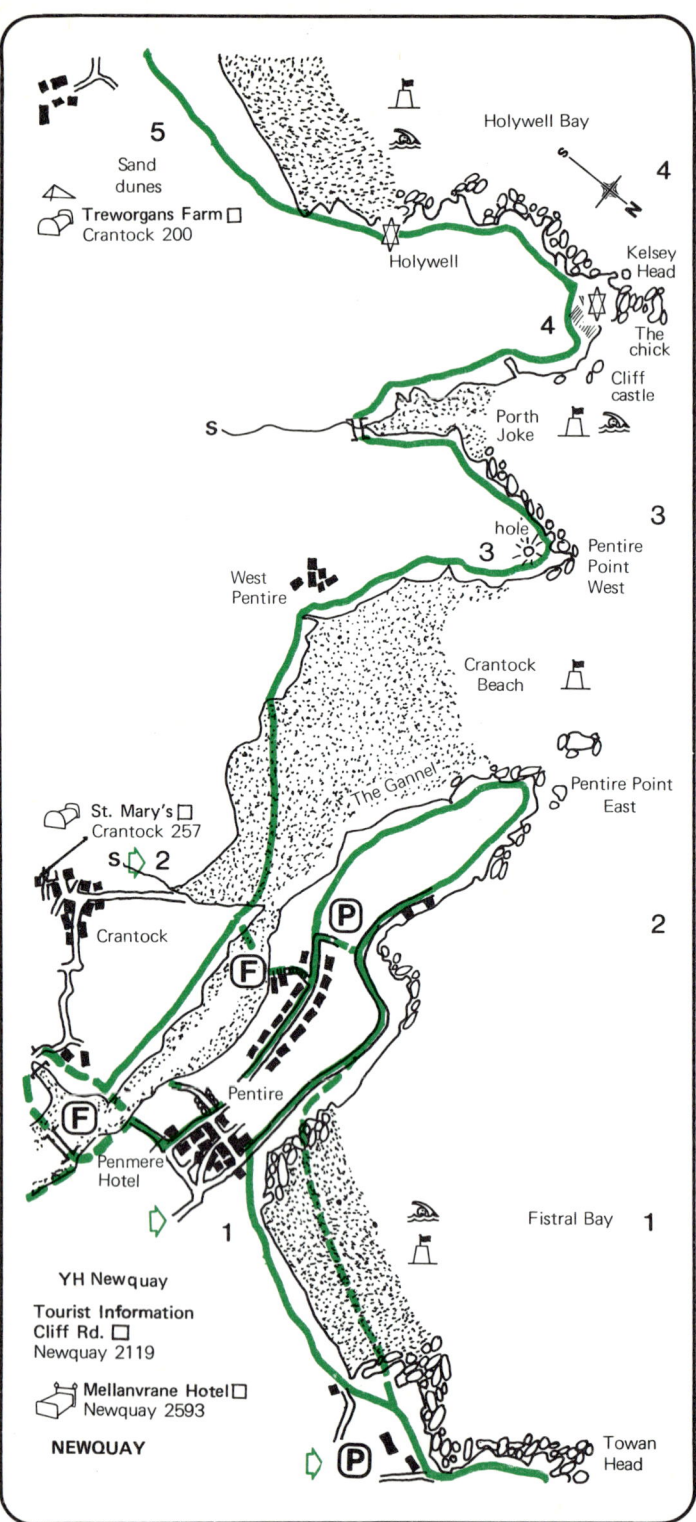

5

Sand dunes

Treworgans Farm
Crantock 200

Holywell Bay

4

Holywell

4

Kelsey Head

The chick

Cliff castle

Porth Joke

3

hole

3

Pentire Point West

West Pentire

Crantock Beach

The Gannel

Pentire Point East

St. Mary's
Crantock 257

S 2

Crantock

2

P

F

Pentire

F

Penmere Hotel

1

Fistral Bay

1

YH Newquay

Tourist Information
Cliff Rd.
Newquay 2119

Mellanvrane Hotel
Newquay 2593

NEWQUAY

P

Towan Head

32. Fistral Bay (Newquay)-Holywell

5½ miles 8¾km   From Minehead 133¾ miles 215¼km

Going: once you get over the Gannel river, pleasant, easy walking.

To get on the Coast Path from the Harbour in Newquay take the steps leading up the cliffs from the north side of the quay; this will bring you out on a roadway which encircles a large hotel (the Huer's House is on your right). The Path starts by the War Memorial and leads over the grass to Towan Head. If you do not wish to go to the end of Towan Head, turn south from the old lifeboat house, along the fence of the large Headlands Hotel. The Path runs above Fistral Beach, following the boundary of the golf course. From Fistral Bay, follow the road at first and then the path going around Pentire Point East. Turn right down steep steps in Riverside Crescent near Fern Pit Café to get to the ferry. A second ferry operates at the bottom of the steep lane that goes off Pentire Crescent by the Penmere Hotel (summer only, whenever tide permits). Shout 'Ferry' and it should appear! (A few yards upstream from this ferry, you can walk across at low tide by two footbridges over the channels.)

The ferry service runs regularly every day from the end of May to September. If you are walking outside this period it is best to take a bus from Newquay to Trevemper Bridge and follow the lane and footpath to Penpol and Crantock Beach.

Above Crantock Beach the Coast Path across the sand dunes is not clear but make for the flagpole and you will then see the track leading to the south side of the beach (you can also keep to the beach). The Path runs between the gardens of some houses and the edge of the low cliff, then alongside fields to Pentire Point West. Once round the Point you come down to a delightful spot, Porth Joke, an unspoiled cove. A rather steep climb up the other side brings you to Kelsey Head. *There is an Iron Age cliff castle on Kelsey Head with a single rampart. Traces of huts have been found in the enclosure. Holywell Bay, a fine sandy surfing beach, has a cave with a spring on the north side of the beach, thought in the old days to have curative properties. The village is an unattractive bungalow growth, relieved by the pub, the Treguth which is 600 years old.*

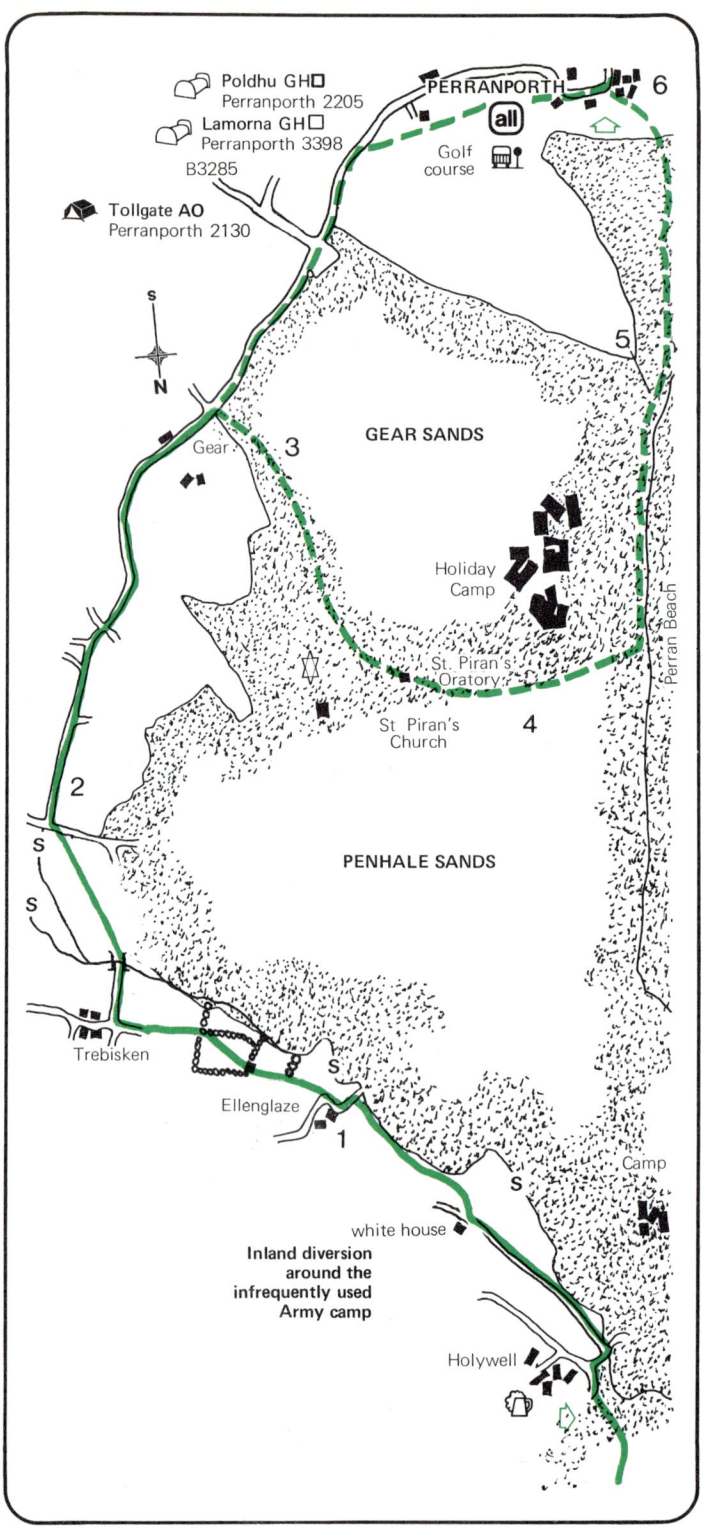

Poldhu GH□
Perranporth 2205
Lamorna GH□
Perranporth 3398
B3285

Tollgate AO
Perranporth 2130

PERRANPORTH 6

all

Golf
course

GEAR SANDS 3

Gear

5

Holiday
Camp

Perran Beach

St. Piran's
Oratory 4

St Piran's
Church

2

PENHALE SANDS

S

S

1

Trebisken

S

Ellenglaze

1

Camp

S

white house

Inland diversion
around the
infrequently used
Army camp

Holywell

33. Holywell-Perranporth
6 miles 9½km   From Minehead 139¾ miles 224¾km

Going: owing to the Penhale military camp occupying a stretch of the coast at Penhale Point the Coast Path, at the time of writing, has to take a detour inland. Quite a pleasant path for most of the way but some road walking necessary.

The diverted Coast Path runs at first along a metalled private road beside the east bank of the stream flowing under the bridge at Holywell. The road after passing one or two houses becomes a pleasant country footpath by the stream. On the right is the north limit of the vast area of sand dunes extending to Perranporth, Penhale Sands. The Path turns away from the stream and passes by Ellenglaze, one of the oldest farmsteads in the county, then over a field and along a farm track which skirts Trebisken, another farm. (After Ellenglaze when crossing the field keep straight on and do not drop down to the stream.) After Trebisken the route turns back towards the stream which is crossed by a footbridge. Diagonally across the field from the footbridge is a gate on to the road. You will have to walk along the road for 1 mile before you turn off to the right following a track signposted to St Piran's Oratory. The route is marked by white stones across the gorse covered heath.

The chapel to which special significance is attached by the Church in Cornwall, is 8th century and has had to be enclosed in a bunker-like building to protect it from encroaching sands. The chapel may be on the site of the cell of St Piran, Irish missionary and patron saint. A short distance to the north-east across the dunes is the site of the 12th-century St Piran's church, and a granite Cross of which there is a 10th-century documentary mention.

The Path continues towards the sea just north of the modern cross on the dunes near the chapel, but most people will prefer to walk along the fine wide sands for the 2 miles to Perranporth, rather than follow the Path through the sand hills. *Perranporth (Port of Piran), an attractive small resort with 3 miles of fine sands and surfing. The church is the third on the site.*

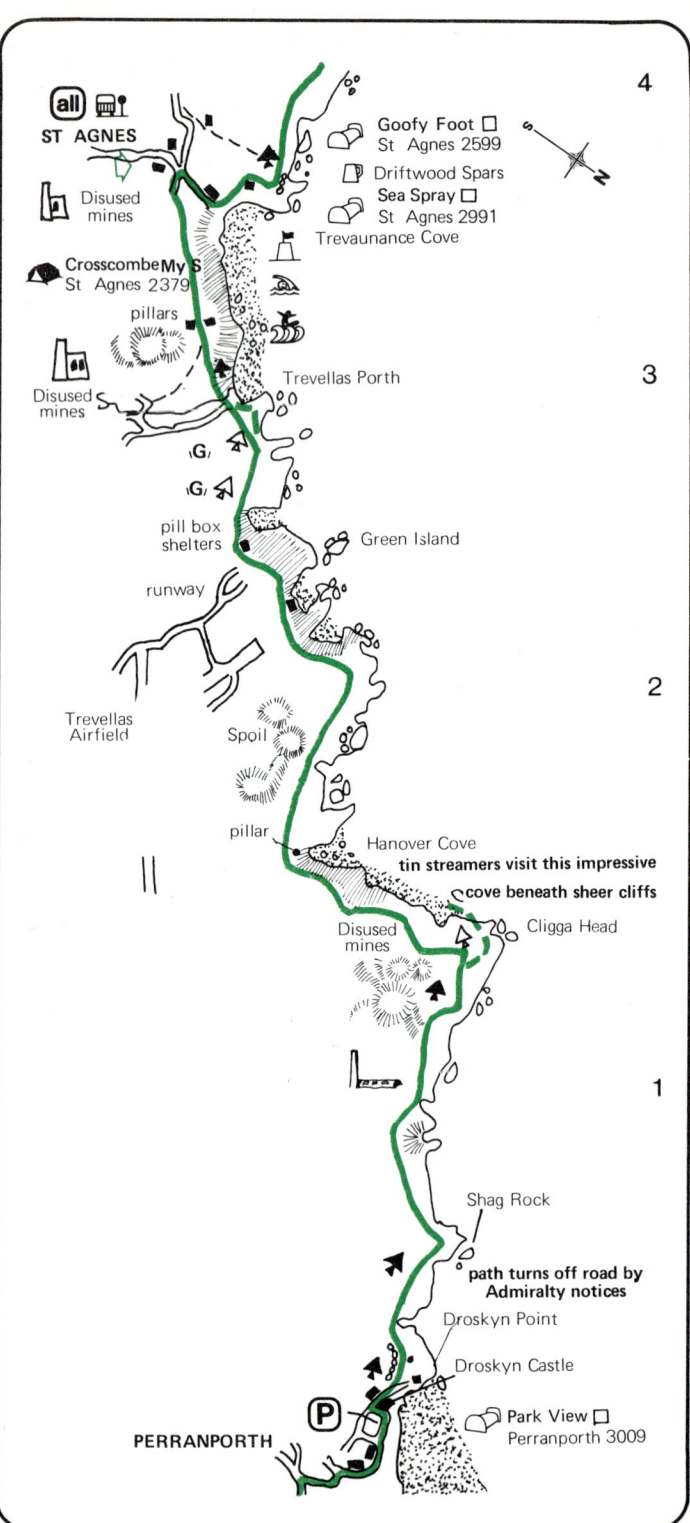

ST AGNES

Disused mines

Goofy Foot ☐
St Agnes 2599

Driftwood Spars
Sea Spray ☐
St Agnes 2991

Trevaunance Cove

Crosscombe My S
St Agnes 2379

pillars

Disused mines

Trevellas Porth

G

G

pill box shelters

Green Island

runway

Trevellas Airfield

Spoil

pillar

Hanover Cove

tin streamers visit this impressive
cove beneath sheer cliffs

Disused mines

Cligga Head

Shag Rock

path turns off road by
Admiralty notices

Droskyn Point

Droskyn Castle

Park View ☐
Perranporth 3009

PERRANPORTH

34. Perranporth-St Agnes

4 miles 6½km   From Minehead 143¾ miles 231¼km

Going: fine cliff walking through what used to be a flourishing copper and tin mining area. Spectacular views.

Take the road which climbs up along the south side of Perran Beach. A path takes you on to a road past the large Droskyn Castle Hotel and towards a fenced naval installation. At the side of the fence a narrow path leads up to the heath-covered cliff top, round Droskyn Point and along the cliff, 250ft above the sea, with a sheer drop below.

On Cligga Head the Path passes through a disused quarry area with large boulders showing the strata of the granite. Just inland is a former RAF airfield now used by Flying and Gliding Clubs.

As the Path twists and turns following the indentations of the coast there are several spots where you can stop to absorb the spellbinding scene of cliff and turbulent sea below.

From here southwards, on the Path, there is much evidence— abandoned mine shafts and engine houses—of the former flourishing copper and tin mining activity: most mines had only a few years of life during the second half of the 19th century.

The descent down to Trevellas Porth, with its ruined mine, is steep as is the ascent the other side. After the scramble up from Trevellas Porth, there is a drop down almost at once to Trevaunance Cove which is the nearest beach to St Agnes, ¾ mile up the road inland.

Trevaunance Cove, formerly a small harbour, had all its installations swept away by storms. Sandy beach and surfing. There is a pub on the waterfront.

St Agnes, with its precipitous streets, derelict mines and rows of houses, homes of miners 100 years ago, is now a place for retired folk and holidaymakers. It has considerable charm, part of which is Stippy Stappy Lane, the name probably meaning very steep. Four good pubs.

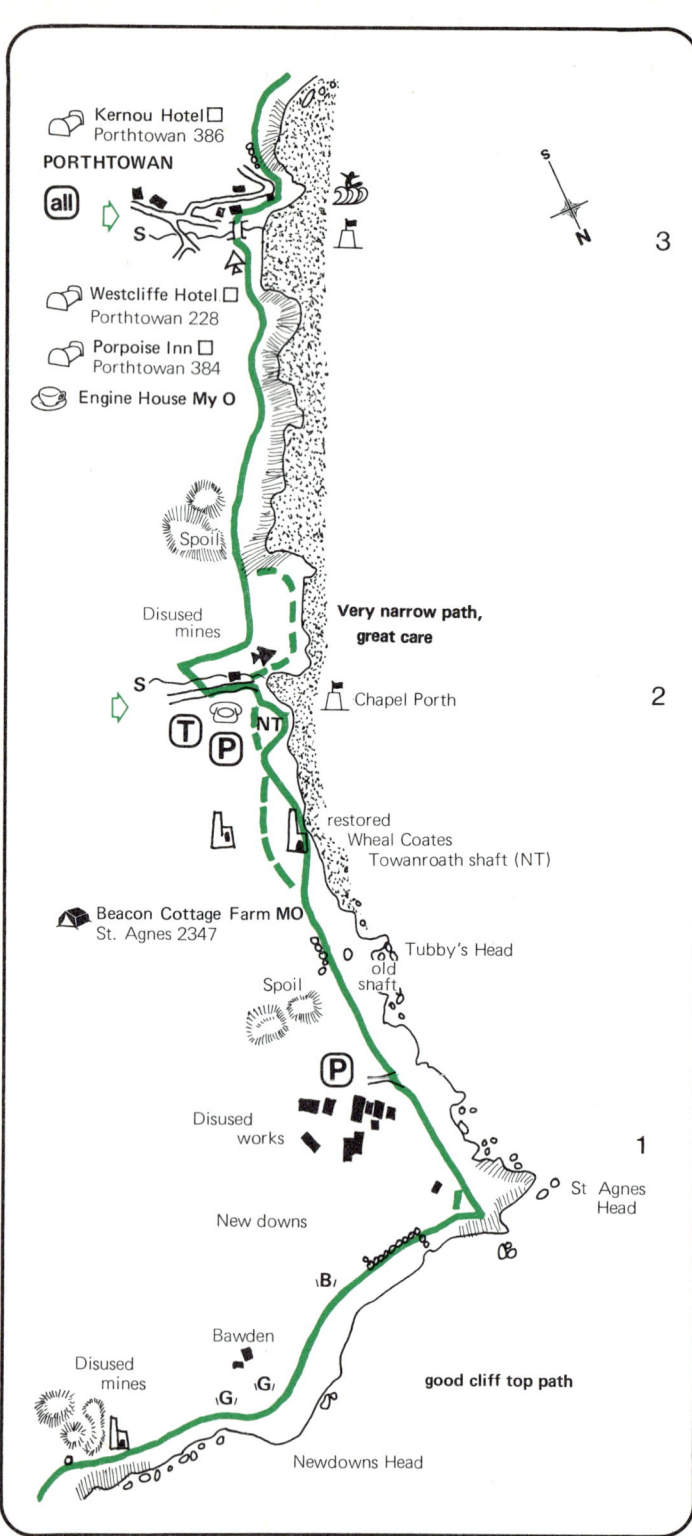

Kernou Hotel □
Porthtowan 386

PORTHTOWAN

all

S

Westcliffe Hotel □
Porthtowan 228

Porpoise Inn □
Porthtowan 384

Engine House My O

Spoil

Disused
mines

**Very narrow path,
great care**

S

T

P

NT

Chapel Porth

restored
Wheal Coates
Towanroath shaft (NT)

Beacon Cottage Farm MO
St. Agnes 2347

Spoil

Tubby's Head

old
shaft

P

Disused
works

St Agnes
Head

New downs

\B/

Bawden

\G/

\G/

Disused
mines

good cliff top path

Newdowns Head

3

2

1

35. Newdowns Head-Porthtowan

$3\frac{1}{2}$ miles $5\frac{1}{2}$ km From Minehead $147\frac{1}{4}$ miles $236\frac{3}{4}$ km

Going: more grand cliff walking on a part of the coast noted for its wildlife.

Rounding St Agnes Head you have a fine view of the cliffs with the occasional gaunt ruins of an engine house or mine workings.

A milder attraction of this part of the coast is the wild life and the flora. St Agnes Head itself has the largest breeding colony of kittiwakes in the area, estimated at 900 pairs. Other breeding sea-birds on the cliffs: herring gull, fulmar, and guillemot. Grey seals can be seen at most times, basking or 'bottling' (standing up in the water, watching the watcher!). In the summer there could be the harmless basking shark. Autumn birds in passage that you might see over the water include skuas, petrels, shearwaters, and diving gannets. Among the flowers that add colour to the scene are thrift, sea campion, birdsfoot trefoil, and spring squill. Grayling and common blue butterflies feed on the vegetation in which lurk lizards and even adders which make off quickly when they detect footsteps.

Passing the engine house of the Towanroath Mine perched below the cliff top we then come to Chapel Porth (National Trust) with a sandy cove between high rocks. A fine expanse of sand is left by the retreating tide.

There is a Chapel Porth Nature Trail, and a leaflet obtainable at the car park provides a fascinating catalogue of the immense variety to be encountered on the Trail: birds, flowers, and plants, insects, mammals, as well as the history of the valley. Conducted tours take place in the summer.

The disused Wheal Charlotte mine lies near the Path as Porthtowan is reached.

Porthtowan is a 'developing' resort and has a sandy beach. Surfing. Two pubs.

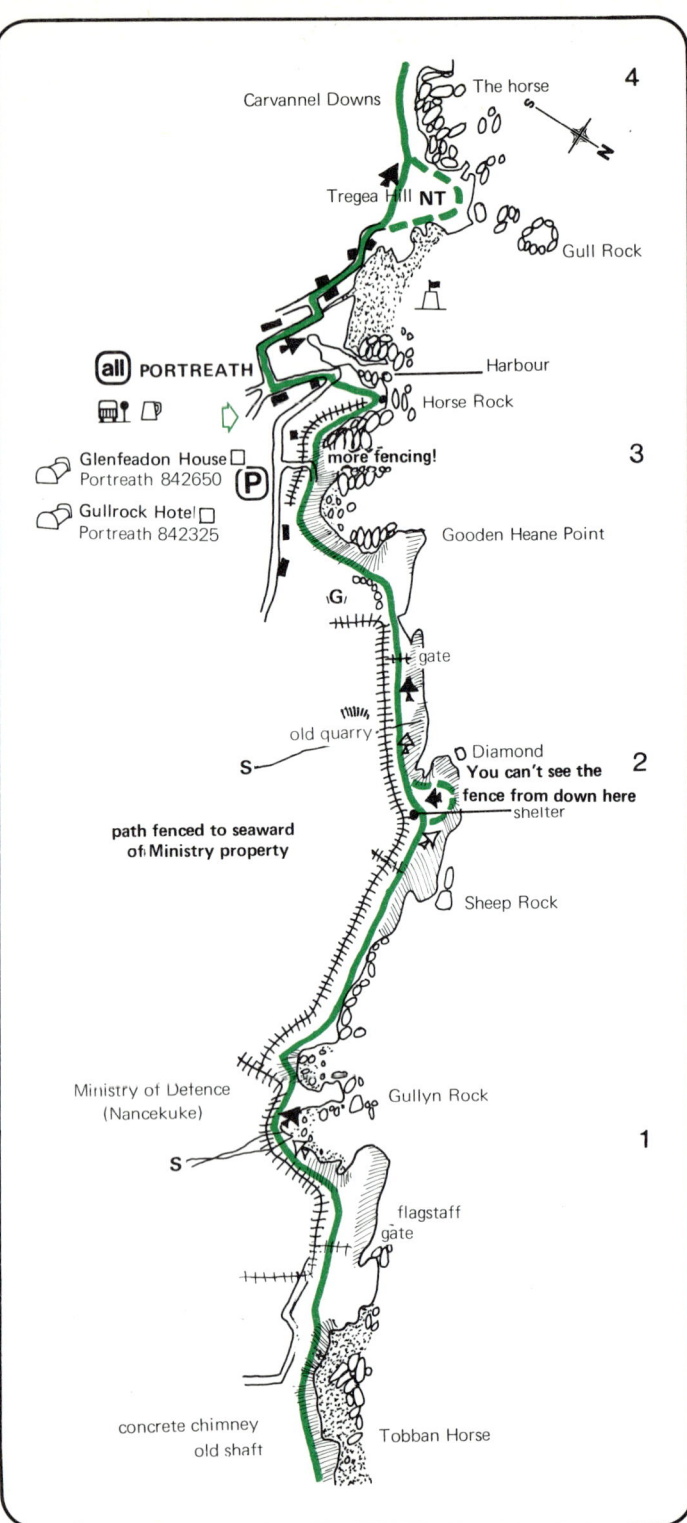

Carvannel Downs

The horse

Tregea Hill **NT**

Gull Rock

(all) PORTREATH

Harbour

Horse Rock

Glenfeadon House
Portreath 842650

more fencing!

Gooden Heane Point

Gullrock Hotel
Portreath 842325

P

\G/

gate

old quarry

S

Diamond

**You can't see the
fence from down here**

shelter

**path fenced to seaward
of Ministry property**

Sheep Rock

Ministry of Defence
(Nancekuke)

Gullyn Rock

S

flagstaff
gate

concrete chimney
old shaft

Tobban Horse

36. Tobban Horse-Portreath-Carvannel Downs

4 miles 6½km   From Minehead 151¼ miles 243¼km

Going: having to walk along the cliff a few inches from the high fence of the Nancekuke Defence Area for more than 1 mile reduces enjoyment but the other parts are pleasant enough and the going good. Two stiff climbs.

From Porthtowan the route of the Path will be seen climbing easily to the cliff top, at first along a by-road, from which the footpath branches off towards the sea. The cliffs drop sheer from 200–250ft as you pass above the little headland, Tobban Horse, and past some mine shafts. Shortly afterwards you have to drop down steeply to the bottom of a cleft, where the stream makes a small waterfall. A scramble up the other side and you encounter the forbidding high fence of the Nancekuke Defence Area. The path hugs the fence for about 2 miles, sometimes wedged narrowly between the fence and the cliff edge. At one point the track becomes incertain but keep as close to the fence as possible as there is no way down the cliff.

Eventually the fence boundary is reached. The Path continues to the entrance road of the Defence Establishment: you can either follow this road down into Portreath or the Path by the car park, round the cliff, past the Daymark tower, to the town.

Portreath is another former busy harbour, serving the mining area of nearby Redruth, now a resort with good sands and a surfing beach. Two pubs: the Portreath and the Basset (the Basset family owned most of the land in the area). The new housing area near the harbour is, for once, most attractive. If you want to see a working tin-streaming operation you can visit the Tolgus Tin Mill at Bridge, 1½ miles up the main road to Redruth (there is a bus). Here you can see the whole process, similar to that used in Cornwall for almost 3000 years.

To rejoin the Coast Path take the narrow country road leading off the main road to the south of the harbour. This leads past some pleasant houses to a footpath climbing through a green valley and round Tregea Hill to the cliff. From here for 6 miles west is National Trust land.

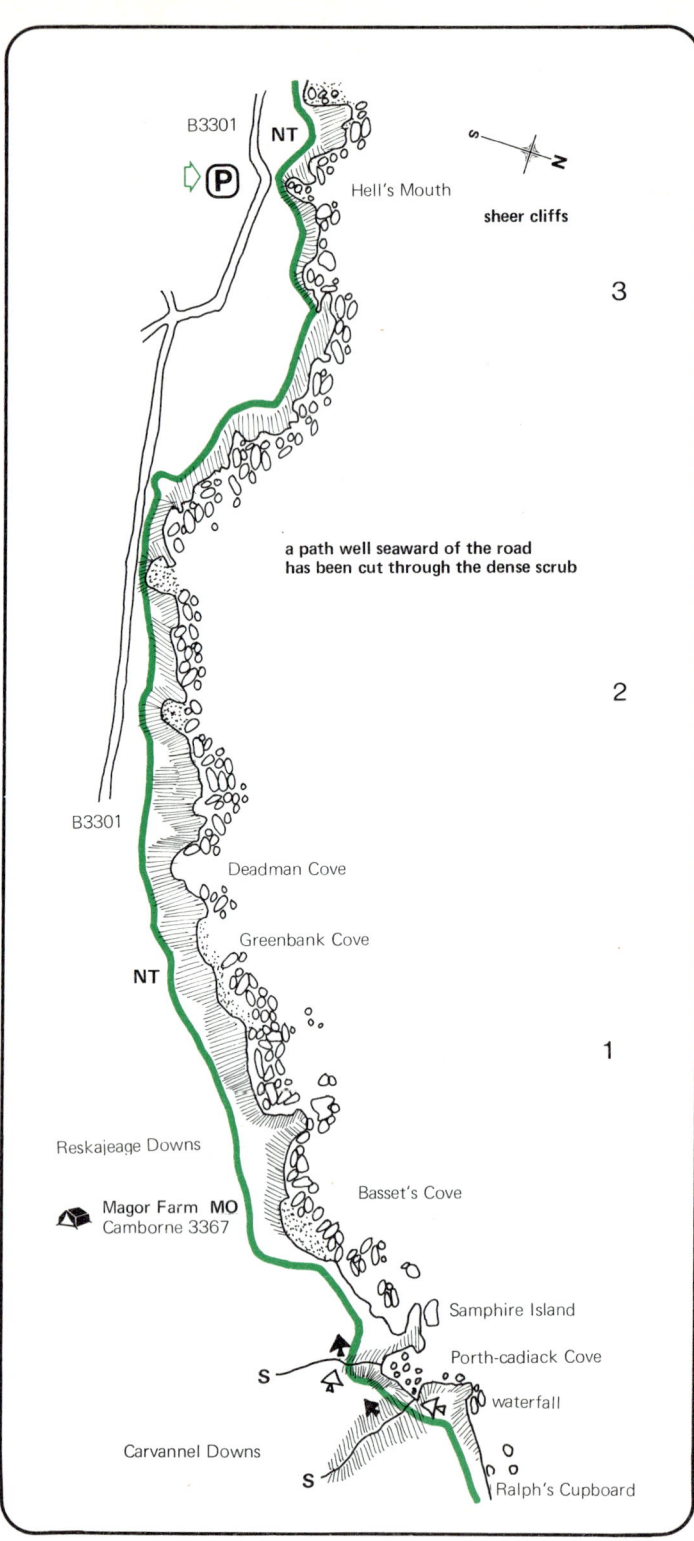

B3301

NT

P

Hell's Mouth

sheer cliffs

3

a path well seaward of the road
has been cut through the dense scrub

2

B3301

Deadman Cove

Greenbank Cove

NT

1

Reskajeage Downs

Magor Farm MO
Camborne 3367

Basset's Cove

Samphire Island

S

Porth-cadiack Cove

S

waterfall

Carvannel Downs

S

Ralph's Cupboard

37. Carvannel Downs-Hell's Mouth

4 miles 6½km   From Minehead 155¼ miles 249¾km

Going: good cliff walking.

There is a steep drop into a cove with a small stream and waterfall. This part of the cliffs is known as Carvannel Downs. *Below the cliff at the head of a narrow inlet, before reaching Carvannel Downs, a cave, Ralph's Cupboard, was used as a smuggler's storehouse.*

Samphire Island, just off the coast, was formerly the source of samphire, gathered for food and pickling.

Carvannel Downs give way to Reskajeage Downs and the Coast Path continues over gorse and turf along this splendid stretch of high cliff. To the west of Samphire Island is Basset's Cove, accessible by a steep path.

About 1 mile farther on, the main road runs close to the cliff edge but a track has been made to take the Coast Path away from the road. The route then turns and follows the coast over the gorse until reaching the awe-inspiring cleft, Hell's Mouth. You will usually find a number of sightseers here in the season as the road is so near.

From Hell's Mouth the Path turns north-west to Navax Point.

Navax Point is another good spot for observing birds in passage usually flying west in the summer and autumn, sometimes in large numbers, particularly shearwaters, gannets, and fulmars. The caves below the Point are breeding places for the grey seal, and the cliffs themselves notable for flowers and plants.

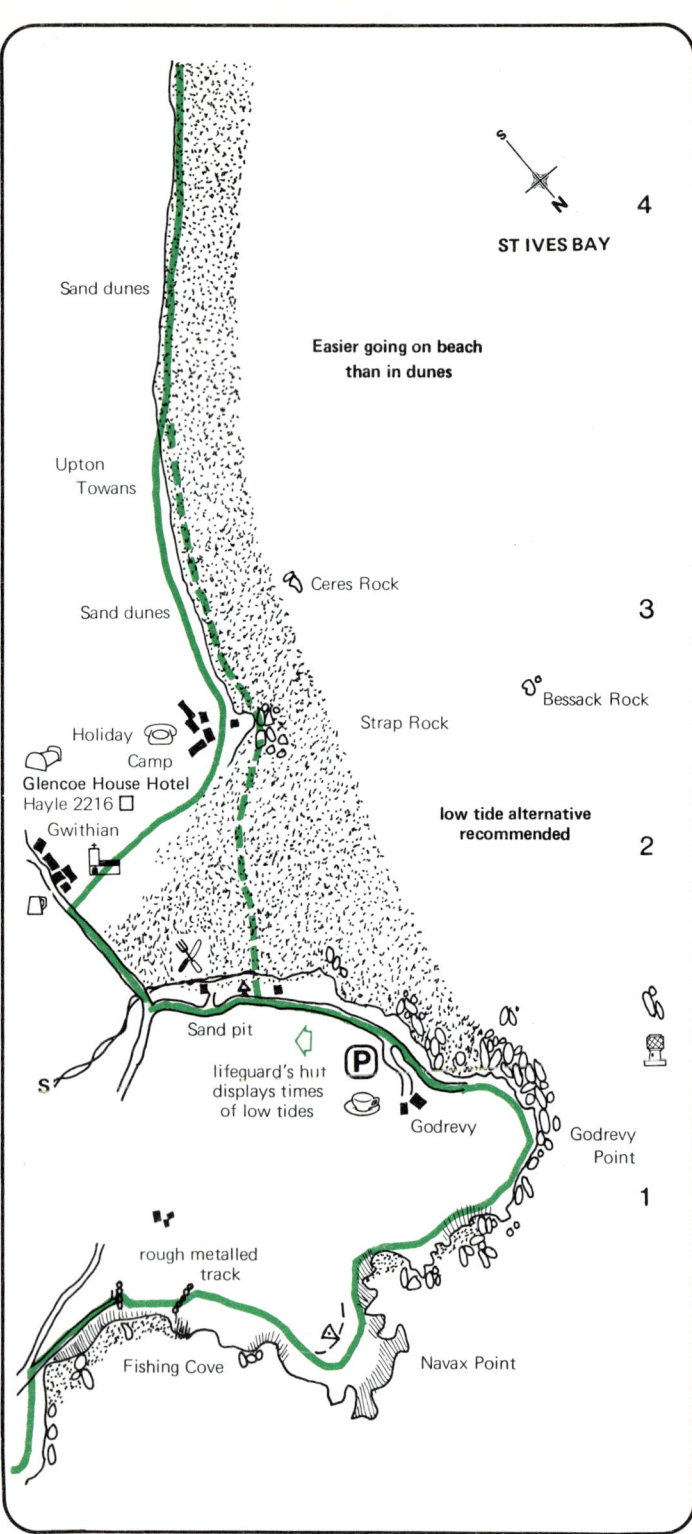

ST IVES BAY

4

Sand dunes

Easier going on beach
than in dunes

Upton
Towans

Sand dunes

Ceres Rock

3

Bessack Rock

Holiday

Camp

Strap Rock

Glencoe House Hotel
Hayle 2216

low tide alternative
recommended

2

Gwithian

Sand pit

S

lifeguard's hut
displays times
of low tides

P

Godrevy

Godrevy
Point

1

rough metalled
track

Navax Point

Fishing Cove

38. Navax Point-Godrevy Point-The Towans (Hayle)

4¾ miles 7¾km   From Minehead 160 miles 257½km

Going: a pleasant short walk round Godrevy Point, a detour inland, and the start of an uninspiring trudge of 2½ miles along the sands of St Ives Bay.

As you follow the path round Godrevy Point, with the unmanned automatic lighthouse on Godrevy Island, the scene may look peaceable enough in the summer but the Stones, a dangerous reef just below the surface, were the cause of many frightful wrecks before the lighthouse was built in 1859—and some even after that. The combination of northerly gales and the Stones usually proved fatal. One sensational wreck was in 1649 : a ship crammed with the possessions of the refugee Prince of Wales, later Charles II, on the day his father was executed, sank on the rocks losing all but three of her crew. People on shore enriched themselves with the loot. Perhaps the most tragic in recent times was that of one of the earliest screw packet steamers, the Nile, which went down on the reef in 1854 with all its passengers and crew.

Having rounded the Point the Path turns inland at the mouth of the stream, the Red River, so named from the red staining from waste of the mines of Redruth. There is a car park and refreshment hut at the National Trust boundary. The Path comes out on the road leaving you to walk ½ mile along it to the charming village of Gwithian with its thatched cottages and old church in whose churchyard lie many victims of shipwrecks in St Ives Bay. Pub: the Pendarves Arms.

A footpath runs seaward by the side of a cottage opposite the church and brings you to a holiday camp site and the beach, popular for surfing and water ski-ing. The Towans (dunes) are dotted with holiday bungalows, chalets, and caravans of no particular attraction but the sands are pleasant ones on a fine day. The Path runs above the high-water mark but most will prefer to walk on the firmer sand.

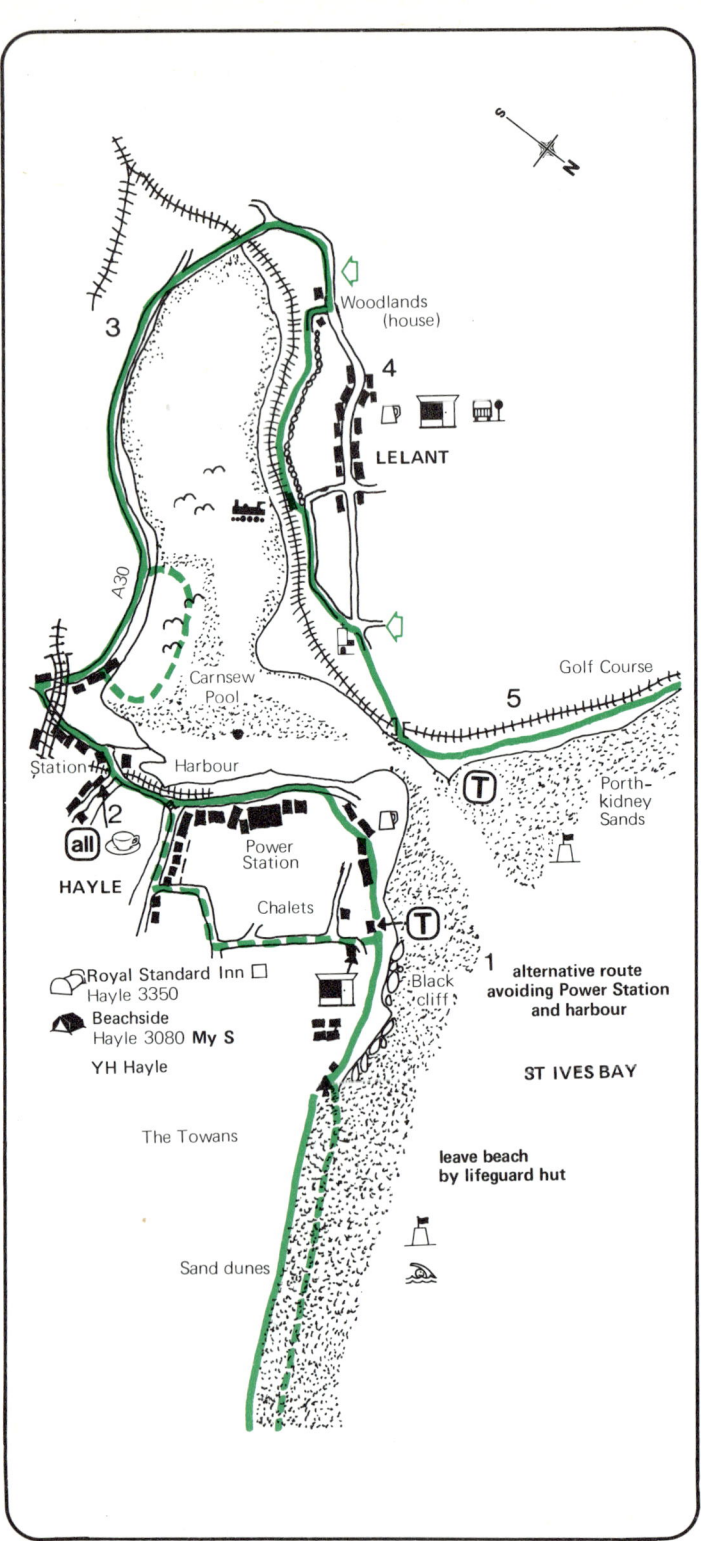

3

Woodlands
(house)

4

LELANT

Golf Course

5

A30

Carnsew
Pool

Porth-
kidney
Sands

Station

Harbour

T

2

all

Power
Station

HAYLE

Chalets

T

1

alternative route
avoiding Power Station
and harbour

Black
cliff

Royal Standard Inn
Hayle 3350

ST IVES BAY

Beachside
Hayle 3080 My S

YH Hayle

leave beach
by lifeguard hut

The Towans

Sand dunes

39. The Towans-Hayle-Porthkidney Sands
5¾ miles 9¼km From Minehead 165¾ miles 266¾km

Going: with the exception of the last mile, this section is through the unprepossessing industrial and harbour area of Hayle. Relief is provided—for those interested—by the many birds to be seen in the Hayle estuary and creeks.

At the far (west) end of the sands (the Towans) is a bungalow town. The Path skirts this, continuing round the dormant power-station, over the canal bridge and on to the busy main road at Hayle. You have no alternative but to walk along this road round the estuary to Lelant. The Path does provide a short diversion presumably because of the bird interest, round Carnsew Pool (see below). There is a bus service (summer) from Hayle to St Ives; also a rail service (from St Erth). At Phillack, ½ mile east of the canal bridge, there is a youth hostel.

Most of the road walk is round the head of the estuary and this provides a good view of the birds, mostly sea-birds and waders, to be seen there. There is also the totally enclosed pool, Carnsew Pool, round which the Path makes a diversion (the footpath sign comes just after the second railway bridge). The Path here provides some quiet and rewarding bird watching. There is a helpful pamphlet Bird Watching at Hayle Estuary *to be had (10p) from the RSPB representative, Tregwyn, Tregye Road, Carnon Downs, Truro. Truro Museum also has copies.*

Continuing along the road, turn up the A3074 towards Lelant. A short way up the hill the Path takes a turning on the right by a roadside cross down a pleasant by-road which brings you along the railway and the shore of the estuary. Past the little Lelant Halt you come to Green Lane and Lelant church.

The church of St Uny is mainly 15th century but has earlier parts including a fine Norman arch. There are two ancient Cornish crosses in the churchyard. St Ives used to come under St Uny parish.

Leaving the churchyard the Path crosses the golf course and goes under a railway bridge before turning along the railway above Porthkidney Sands, dangerous for bathing but a good place for sea birds, including terns, in the autumn.

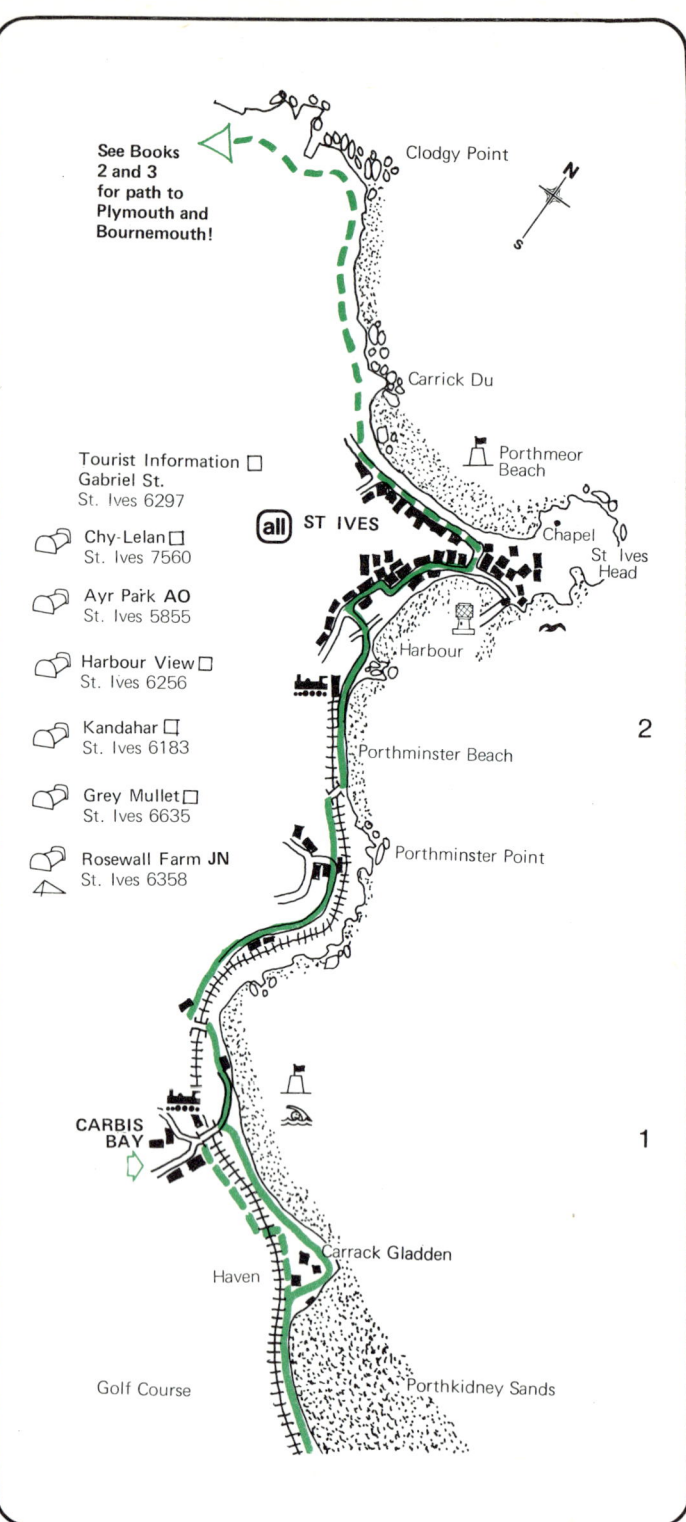

See Books
2 and 3
for path to
Plymouth and
Bournemouth!

Clodgy Point

N

S

Carrick Du

Tourist Information □
Gabriel St.
St. Ives 6297

Porthmeor
Beach

all ST IVES

Chapel

Chy-Lelan □
St. Ives 7560

St Ives
Head

Ayr Park **AO**
St. Ives 5855

Harbour View □
St. Ives 6256

Harbour

Kandahar □
St. Ives 6183

2

Grey Mullet □
St. Ives 6635

Porthminster Beach

Rosewall Farm **JN**
St. Ives 6358

Porthminster Point

1

CARBIS
BAY

Carrack Gladden

Haven

Golf Course

Porthkidney Sands

88

40. Porthkidney Sands-St Ives
2¼ miles 3½km   From Minehead 168 miles 270¼km

Going: this short last section takes you along a good cliff path overlooking St Ives Bay and then into the resort itself.

From above Porthkidney Beach, the Coast Path proceeds alongside the railway until Carbis Bay station where it takes to the roadway leading down past the Carbis Bay Hotel. Once past the Hotel the Path goes over the railway and follows it closely, crossing over the line again, and drops down to Porthminster Beach and the Harbour.

St Ives (pop 9700). One of the best known Cornish resorts. In the older parts of the town fishermen's cottages are packed closely up the slope from the harbour, and above are those of the miners who worked in the nearby mines in the 1800s. On the high ground, along the approaches from the south are the prosperous villas and hotels of the residential quarter, enjoying fine views over the sea. The town is named after St Ia, daughter of an Irish chieftain, who landed here in AD 460 on a Christian mission. An established fishing town by the 14th century it was granted in 1487 by Henry VII the right to hold a market and two fairs. Its livelihood depended on pilchard fishing, and when this declined in the 1890s the coming of the railway made it a popular holiday and residential town—a favourite with artists. The parish church of St Ia is 15th century and on St Ives Head (still called The Island although joined to the mainland for some centuries) there is the ruined chapel of St Nicholas, the seafarer's saint. Smeaton, famous builder of the Eddystone Lighthouse, constructed the harbour in 1770. Museum and Information Bureau. Terminus of the short branch line from St Erth on the main London–Penzance line. Bus station. Four excellent beaches: on the east Porthminster, Carbis Bay, and Porthgwidden; on the north, Porthmeor (surfing). St Ives Head is a fine spot for bird-watching, especially during the autumn and spring migrations.

History

There is mention wherever possible, in the text accompanying the sketch-maps, of historical monuments, prehistoric sites etc. on the Path but these short notes are to give a general historical background to your walk.

In Kent's Cavern in Torquay traces have been found of Palaeolithic (Old Stone Age) Man of 12,000 years ago, the earliest in the south-west; and in the Land's End area there are the stone chamber tombs of the Neolithic (New Stone Age) era going back 5,000 years or more. These tomb builders came from the Atlantic seaboard of the Continent—probably in coracles, as still used in parts of Ireland—and they raised crops, reared animals, and made pottery. In about 2000 BC the more advanced Beaker Folk arrived who were able to work metals. Five hundred years later Bronze Age man, living mainly by agriculture, found how to make tools and weapons more effective by adding tin to copper. Dating from this period are the fine gold lunulae or crescent-shaped ornaments found in Harlyn (section 28), probably from Ireland, indicating trade with other places.

The most significant wave of migrants to the south-west was that of Iron Age Celts in about 700 BC, a tall, strong warlike people from north-west Europe, from whose language Cornish and the other Celtic languages were derived. The many cliff castles on our Path were from this time; steep headlands were fortified by high ramparts and deep ditches, probably built as a defensive foothold on landing, and a rear base for later advances. Trevelgue Head near Newquay (section 31) is the most impressive. These Celts worked in metals, making bronze utensils and ornaments. They wove textiles and their pottery was of artistic design. Tin was smelted and exported to the Mediterranean, probably through St Michael's Mount.

The Romans who landed in AD 43 stopped short at Isca Dumnoniorum (Exeter), after subduing the local Celts now called the Dumnonii. The two Roman sites on the Coast Path, Old Barrow near Wingate (section 4) and Martinhoe (section 7), were military signal stations of AD 45–75. Watch was kept on raiding tribes from the Welsh coast opposite who were not conquered until AD 75. Signal fires were lit to warn the cruising Roman fleet of raids. Farther west there are only a few Roman sites: one or two milestones, and a few villas. Cornwall was a poor land and the few inhabitants not likely to bother the Romans.

After the departure of the Romans in AD 410 the Romano-British left behind were forced into Wales and Cornwall by the many waves of Anglo-Saxon invaders, some crossing the Channel to join their fellow-Celts in 'Brittany'. The Saxons increased their hold on the country over the following 400 years. The Dumnonii of Devon were overcome in 710, but those of Cornwall continued unmolested under their own kings, keeping their language and culture. The former boundary between Saxon Devon and Celtic Cornwall can be traced from the Cornish place-names which have survived. They start with the higher ground near Poundstock along the River Ottery down to Launceston. So when you cross Wanson Mouth on the Coast Path (section 19) you are crossing the old boundary behind which the Cornish kept their identity for so long. It was not until after Athelstan subdued Cornwall in 932 that the present boundary was fixed along the Tamar, bringing places with Saxon names like Kilkhampton into the county.

The 5th–6th centuries were remarkable for the number of Welsh, Irish, and Breton missionaries who came over, giving their names to the churches, towns, and villages: St Kew, St Hya, St Petroc, etc. On the site of their cells churches were built. From this period survive many old Cornish crosses found in churchyards near the Path. Some are memorials to local chieftains, and the inscriptions in Latin indicate that the aristocratic structure and something of Roman culture survived, as well as their faith. An example is the Selus Stone in St Just church. St Piran's Chapel near Perranporth (section 33) is an ancient site much revered by the Cornish.

The Normans landed in 1066, and by 1072 had the south-west in their hands. Their barons, among whom the land was divided, built castles around which towns sprang up. Other towns followed as markets were set up by traders in the wake of the Conquest. The villages and towns on the Coast Path started as fishing villages and some grew because of the facilities they offered for trading overseas. Tin continued to be extracted from alluvial sources, and from the 13th century these stanneries, under a Warden, received royal charters. The tin was tested at official coinage towns: Truro, Bodmin, Lostwithiel, Liskeard, and Helston—'coinage' is derived from the old French word for the stamp impressed on the ingots after assay.

As with the rest of the country the structure of the West was feudal; the land was owned by a few powerful families who led their tenants and peasants to Agincourt, the Crusades, and later to man the ships and fortifications against Spain in the days of Elizabeth. Typical of West Country leaders was Sir Richard Grenville of Stowe (section 17).

In 1497 Cornishmen marched to London to protest against Henry VII's taxes, many being killed; in 1459 Devon and Cornwall, in revolt against Henry VIII's church reforms, besieged protestant Exeter, many being executed after defeat. Again, in 1688 Cornishmen marched on Bristol when Bishop Trelawney was put in the Tower for opposing James II.

In the Civil War most of the Cornish gentry were for the King but Devon and Somerset were divided. Led by Hopton and Bevil Grenville, a descendant of Sir Richard, the Cornish contingent fought many brave engagements, defeating the Roundheads at Stamford Hill, near Bude (section 18), Braddock Downs, and Lansdown (Bath) where Sir Bevil was killed.

Fishing was always the major occupation on the coast but from 1700 onwards the mining of copper as well as tin grew into a thriving industry. Land's End and the Redruth area were the main centres but on the Coastal Path near St Agnes (section 34 and 35) there are traces of intense mining activity. The copper boom lasted from the mid-1800s to 1870 until killed by competition from Australia and other places overseas; tin mining was also affected by Malayan development and seriously declined. Hundreds of miners were thrown out of work; many emigrating to the new mining areas. In the 1890s the pilchard shoals, from which so many fishing villages gained a living, disappeared.

Despite 18th and 19th-century industrial activity, life in Cornwall was hard and the people poor. Bad conditions and drink posed problems but John Wesley's famous Cornwall campaigns (1743–89) brought light and hope into the lives of many as the myriad little chapels testify.

The coming of the railways, which first reached Cornwall in 1859, led to the transformation of picturesque fishing villages and coastal towns into popular resorts, and the thriving tourist industry has hardly looked back since.

Geology

These notes offer elementary general features to add interest to the walk and perhaps encourage the non-expert reader to further study. The geology of any area affects every aspect: the scenery, vegetation, history, buildings, wild life, and the livelihood of those who live there.

The rocks on the south-west coast are predominently Devonian and Carboniferous sediments known by the local miner's term 'killas'. They were formed eons ago on the beds of seas or lakes, and some are fossil-bearing. There are, however, outcrops of igneous rock with no fossils, some of a volcanic type, eg the spectacular pillow lavas forming 250ft-high cliffs at Pentire Head, which affect not only the scenery but also the whole environment. Hard greenstones usually form headlands, eg Park Head, Trevose Head, Stepper Point, and Rumps Point, and were used by Stone Age Man for hand axes.

Sedimentary formations can take many forms but can be described generally as mudstones, sandstones, and limestones—the oldest being about 300 million years old. Immense pressures over the geological ages have twisted and bent the strata into the strange shapes to be seen in the cliffs at Millook Haven (section 19) or the boulders on Bude beach. The many small islands a few yards off the coast often present strata of unusual contortions. These pressures have converted many of the mudstones into slates, eg at Delabole near Trebarwith there is the huge working quarry.

The igneous formations also have various forms; they are rocks which, while in a molten state, have been thrust up into the older sedimentary strata. Deep down in the crust of the earth they then cooled. They have since become exposed by the action of the sea or weather, or both. The granite of the Cornish coast is an example of this.

Such igneous rocks have had the effect of changing the local sedimentary rocks with which they came into contact, both through colossal heat and pressures. These areas of contact are known as metamorphic aureoles, as they form a halo or ring of changed rocks around, for example, the granite. Gases and liquid substances of differing chemical composition were forced into fissures in the local rock, and it is in such areas that the mineral ores of tin, copper, and other metals were found and exploited by the mines of Cornwall.

On the Path you see the tremendous effect of the sea and weather on the coastal landscape over hundreds of millions of years. The sedimentary rocks vary in hardness, and the more resistant often occur with others of less resistance which are more quickly worn by sea and weather leaving isolated pillars of the harder rock, known as sea stacks, as at Bedruthan Steps; long narrow spines of rock jutting out on the beaches, as at Bude, and rock arches, such as Northern Door, north of Boscastle.

Some of the impressive sites round the coast are dry river beds, such as the Valley of the Rocks at Lynton where the sandstones have been weathered to produce fantastic shapes. The sea is still hard at work washing away shore and cliff in many places. A recent tragic phenomenon was the Lynmouth flood disaster of 1952, where the swollen Lyn river brought down hundreds of tons of boulders.

One very obvious geological link is the appearance and composition of the beaches. For example, beaches on the Coast Path east of Woolacombe are of grey sand, the colour of the predominating rock of which the grains of sand are mostly formed. South of Woolacombe the sandstone produces golden sands. Beaches of minute shells make for white beaches. Usually there is a mixture of rock and shell in any beach, with varying proportions. The composition of a particular beach and its exposure to wave action affects the shore life: the plants, molluscs, and so on. These make a fascinating study and we recommend Roger Burrow's book *The Naturalist in Devon and Cornwall*.

Fossils, too, can be found in many places on this stretch of coast, often becoming exposed in the cliffs. More attention is given to this in Book 3 when dealing with the Seaton–Lyme Regis area.

Birds on the coast path

It is not possible to list every bird but perhaps some useful clues can be given which may help the walker and increase his enjoyment. Species likely to be seen depend on the time of year and location. The best times for viewing are the spring, autumn, and winter. Field-glasses are almost a necessity. **Please do not disturb birds especially those at nesting sites.**

The Coast Path takes you over heathland, field and pasture, woodland, sand dunes, and sea shore and on each of these you find in general the same birds as on similar ground in other parts of the country, with a few exceptions. The high cliffs offer shelter and breeding-grounds for some sea birds not seen in other parts of south Britain; the South-west Peninsula, jutting out as it does into the Atlantic, provides a grandstand view of spring and autumn migrants. From the headlands of north Cornwall may be seen, just off-shore, flocks of birds in passage including gannets, Manx shearwaters, petrels, auks, and great and arctic skuas. The estuaries and coastal marshes give food and shelter in the winter to many kinds of duck and wader.

The list below gives the most common birds likely to be seen in the various types of terrain. There is some overlap, both in habitat and season. (*S* = Spring, *Su* = Summer, *A* = Autumn, *W* = Winter.)

Cliff-face Breeding: herring gull, great black-backed gull, fulmar, kittiwake, guillemot, razorbill, jackdaw, carrion crow, raven.

Seashore and rocks herring gull, great black-backed gull, black-headed gull *(W)*, common gull *(W)*, shag, cormorant, common tern *(A)*, oystercatcher, dunlin *(W)*, curlew *(W)*, rock pipit, pied wagtail, turnstone *(AW)*.

Cliff-top *Gorse-covered heath:* wren, stonechat, whitethroat *(Su)*, kestrel, linnet, buzzard, cuckoo, spotted flycatcher *(Su)*, chaffinch, green woodpecker, goldfinch, dunnock. *Open field:* skylark, yellowhammer, corn bunting, lapwing *(W)*, fieldfare *(W)*, redwing *(W)*, swallow *(Su)*, house martin *(Su)*, swift *(Su)*, meadow pipit *(Su)*, magpie, barn owl.

Estuaries redshank, herring gull, great black-backed gull, common gull *(W)*, black-headed gull *(W)*, green shank *(W)*, teal *(W)*, wigeon *(W)*, golden plover *(W)*, mute swan, shelduck, curlew, common tern *(W)*, razorbill, guillemot *(Su)*, black-tailed and bar-tailed godwit *(W)*.

Woodland and Streams song thrush, blackbird, green and great spotted woodpecker, great tit, blue tit, coal tit, nuthatch, tree creeper, goldcrest, jay, cuckoo *(Su)*, chiffchaff, sparrowhawk, tawny owl, moorhen, coot, grey wagtail, dipper, kingfisher.

Less common visitors in summer, also to be seen in passage: redstart, yellow wagtail, blackcap, pied flycatcher. Rarities such as hoopoe and golden oriole are also sometimes seen. Occasional autumn visitors are black redstarts.

In the winter, in estuaries, freshwater pools and marshes the keen bird-watcher may catch sight of grebes—great-crested, red-headed and black-headed; spoonbill; divers—great northern, black-throated and red-throated; duck—eider, red-breasted merganser; geese—barnacle and white-fronted; waders: ruff, knot, spoonbill.

Winter predators include hen harrier, peregrine, and merlin. Ospreys are sometimes seen in the autumn in passage. The purple sandpiper is another regular but never common winter visitor and may be seen dodging the waves while feeding on the rocks.

Areas of particular bird interest (indicated in the sketch maps by a bird symbol)

Baggy Point On cliffs: herring gull, fulmar. Autumn migration of finches, larks, and pipits

Bull Point On cliffs: herring gull, fulmar. Autumn migration of finches, larks and pipits.

Camel Estuary Winter: divers (near mouth)—great northern, black-throated, red-throated; black-headed and common gull; golden plover; knot; mallard; teal; wigeon; shelduck; shoveler; goldeneye; dunlin; black and bar-tailed godwit; Bewick's swan; white-fronted goose. Autumn (mainly): migrating terns. Herring and great black backed gull; oystercatcher; common sandpiper; redshank; shelduck. Occasional: osprey; peregrine. Large heronry south bank

Hartland Point Autumn: migrating finches, larks, etc. In passage off-shore: kittiwake; Manx shearwater; auks and gannets

Hayle Estuary herring and great black-backed gull; oystercatcher; common sandpiper; shelduck; redshank. Winter: black-headed and common gull; golden plover; dunlin; teal; wigeon; goldeneye; lapwing; great northern diver; knot

Lye Rock Cliff nesting in breeding season: herring and great black-backed gull; fulmar; puffin; razorbill; guillemot; shag; cormorant

Porlock Marsh Summer: oystercatcher; dunlin; common sandpiper; redshank; sedge warbler; reed bunting. Winter: teal; wigeon; turnstone; knot; greenshank; green sandpiper; ringed plover

St Agnes Head Cliff nesting in breeding season: kittiwake; herring gull; black-backed gull; fulmar; razorbill; guillemot; shag; cormorant

St Ives Island Fine observation post for migrating birds during strong south-west winds. Flocks include gannet; Manx shearwater; storm and Leach's petrel; great and arctic skua; common, arctic and sandwich tern; common sandpiper; swift

Short and Long Island Cliff nesting in breeding season: herring and great black-backed gull; fulmar; puffin; razorbill; guillemot; shag; cormorant

Flowers and Plants

On this sector of the Coast Path the terrain covered is of ever-changing variety, from moorland of over 1,000ft to three large sand dune areas. The flora displays a similar diversity and the purpose of these short notes is to give to those who already know something of the subject an idea of some of the species likely to be encountered.

Woodland Coppice oak, both sessile and common oaks. Elm thickets including the small-leaved Cornish elm. Introduced and quickly spreading sycamore and ash. Monterey pine grows well in exposed places. Typical flowers: bluebell, lesser celandine, wood sorrel, wood avens, common cow wheat, bilberry (locally called 'urts), golden saxifrage, Cornish moneywort and, rarely, bastard balm. A splendid fern population includes hay-scented buckler fern, royal fern, hard fern, Tunbridge filmy fern, hart's tongue, golden scale male fern and lady fern. Locally stands of introduced turkey and holm oaks withstand well the salt air.

Coastal scrub Locally developed in small valleys and disturbed ground areas. Common species include tamarisk, wild privet, sycamore, European gorse, blackthorn, elder, and brambles. Ground flora very restricted in these places.

Dry heathland *Dominated by western gorse and bell heather* with ling, tormentil, sawwort, betony, madder, dodder, leady hawkweed and a variety of mosses and lichens including Cladonia. *Ling-dominated* areas are often more exposed to the sea and have maritime species including thrift, sea and buck's horn plantain, sea carrot, vernal squill, and centuary, also locally prostrate broom. Other species include bird's foot trefoil, wild thyme, slender-flowered thistle, English stonecrop, carline thistle, and sheep's bit. *Grass-dominated* sward of sheep's fescue and bristle bent grasses with scurvy grass, thrift, bluebell and primroses

Wet heathland Locally bog moss areas with pale butterwort, round and long-leaved sundews, devil's bit scabious, bog pimpernel. Purple moor grass areas with bog rush and royal fern, also purple loosestrife, thrift, and cotton grasses

Rock flora *Natural cliff outcrops:* thrift, common and golden samphire, rock sea spurry, sea beet, sea spleenwort, rock sea lavender, common scurvy grass and early scurvy grass, sea and buck's horn plantain, sea mayweed, sea campion, yellow stonecrop, English stonecrop, wild thyme, penny wort. *Mine heaps:* ling, western and European gorse, tormentil, thrift foxglove, weld, ragwort, southern marsh orchid.

Dunes Marram and sea lyme grass and wide variety of other lime-loving species. Beaked hawk's beard, carline thistle, cowslip, hound's tongue, kidney vetch, ploughman's spikenard, rest harrow, salad burnet, spotted cat's ear, stinking iris, vipers bugloss, wild carrot, yellow wort, stork's bill

Arable and pasture, some rough Ragwort, birds foot trefoil, coltsfoot, mouse-ear chickweed, primrose, winter heliotrope, alexanders, wild teasel, sea mayweed, yellow bartsia, three-cornered leek, yellow rattle, pale flax, rest harrow, foxglove, hairy tare, corn spurrey, common fumitory, corn marigold, red valerian, hogweed and common cat's ear

Bibliography

Automobile Association *Book of the Seaside,* 1972
Burrows R *The Naturalist in Devon and Cornwall,* 1971
Carter C *Cornish Shipwrecks* Vol. 2, North Coast, 1970
Cornwall Archaeological Society *Principal Antiquities of the Newquay-Padstow District,* 1962
Cornwall Bird-Watching and Preservation Society *Annual Report 1974*
Daniell S *The Story of Cornwall,* Tor Mark Press
Dyer J *Southern England, An Archaeological Guide,* 1973
Fox A *South-West England 3500 BC–AD 600,* 1973
Hoskins W G *Devon,* 1974
HMSO *Exmoor National Park,* 1974
National Trust *The National Trust Guide,* 1973
Rowse A L *Sir Richard Grenville of the Revenge,* 1937
Seymour J *The Companion Guide to the Coast of South-West England,* 1974
South-West Way Association *Annual Reports*
Better Pubs, Red Cross House, Crediton, publish map-guides to pubs in E & W Cornwall, S & E Devon, Dorset and Somerset

Acknowledgments

Help has been received from many kind people in compiling this book and this the authors gratefully acknowledge. They would particularly like to mention Roger Burrows, BA, MIBiol of Exeter University for his advice and help over flora, wild life, and geology; Roger Butts of the Cornwall Members' Group of the Royal Society for the Protection of Birds for help on birds; the Countryside Commission, Cheltenham; and HM Coast Guards at Porthgwarra and Wyke Regis.

Anyone walking the Path soon becomes aware of the sterling work done by the National Trust in keeping the area accessible for everyone.

A new organization, the South-west Way Association, is dedicated to furthering the interests of walkers of the South-west Peninsula Coast Path, acting as a watch-dog where access to the Path is threatened and prodding lethargic local authorities into observing their legal responsibility to make available and maintain the section of path in their territories. Details from: 'Kynance', 15, Old Newton Road, Kingskerswell, Newton Abbot, Devon.

Many sources have been used including the works listed in the Bibliography which are recommended for further study. Every care has been taken but conditions are so liable to change that the publishers can assume no responsibility for accuracy.